Praise for *The Five-Y*

"High costs and debt, insufficient instru[c] and poor job prospects: for too many s[tudents the] party often turns into a lifelong nightmare. *The Five-Year Party* is packed with illuminating stories and details about this crisis situation, and helps readers to avoid the dangers and get the most for their money."

—Marc Scheer, Author, *No Sucker Left Behind: Avoiding the Great College Rip-Off*

"In one dismaying and maddening episode and circumstance after another, Craig Brandon's survey of college campuses sounds a vital warning for parents: 'The institutions and administrators you trust to foster and guide your children's formation are more interested in their pocketbooks than their intellects. Buyer beware!'"

—Mark Bauerlein, Author of *The Dumbest Generation: How the Digital Age Stupefies Young Americans and Jeopardizes Our Future* and Professor of English, Emory University

"After reading only a few pages of *The Five-Year Party*, I immediately started telling people about its important message. This crucial book exposes the consumer mentality now all too prevalent on college campuses, detailing how higher education has given students what they *want* at the expense of giving them what they *need* to compete in the global marketplace. Even better, the book tells parents and educators how this nefarious trend can be circumvented. Any parent who wants their college-bound teen to actually learn something for their heaps of tuition money should read this book."

—Jean M. Twenge, Author of *Generation Me* and Co-Author of *The Narcissism Epidemic* and Professor of Psychology, San Diego State University

"With broad, unforgiving strokes, Craig Brandon paints a dark picture of residential college life that will give every parent pause before sending a child off to any of his 'Party Schools.'"

—Barrett Seaman, Author of *Binge: Campus Life in an Age of Disconnection and Excess*

The Five-Year Party

HOW COLLEGES HAVE GIVEN UP ON EDUCATING YOUR CHILD AND WHAT YOU CAN DO ABOUT IT

Craig Brandon

BENBELLA BOOKS, INC.

Dallas, TX

BenBella Books, Inc.
6440 N. Central Expressway, Suite 503
Dallas, TX 75206
www.benbellabooks.com
Send feedback to feedback@benbellabooks.com

Printed in the United States of America
10 9 8 7 6 5 4 3 2 1

Library of Congress Cataloging-in-Publication data is available for this title.
ISBN 978-1935251-80-4

Copyediting by D. L. Kirkby, Kirkby Editorial Services
Proofreading by Erica Lovett and Stacia Seaman
Cover design by Michael Fusco Design
Text design and composition by PerfecType, Nashville, TN
Index by Shoshana Hurwitz
Printed by Bang Printing

Distributed by Perseus Distribution
http://www.perseusdistribution.com/

To place orders through Perseus Distribution:
Tel: (800) 343-4499
Fax: (800) 351-5073
E-mail: orderentry@perseusbooks.com

Significant discounts for bulk sales are available. Please contact
Glenn Yeffeth at glenn@benbellabooks.com or (214) 750-3628.

To my granddaughter,
Charlotte Claire Brandon Anthony:
May you never have to endure the terrors of a party school.

Contents

Introduction

My first inkling that something had gone seriously haywire in higher education came just after the turn of the millennium, when I was asked to take over the job of advisor to the campus radio station. I had spent the previous five years as a full-time journalism instructor and advisor to the student newspaper at Keene State College in New Hampshire, but I knew very little about radio. Nevertheless, it seemed like an interesting challenge and many of my colleagues from the College Media Advisors, who advised both newspapers and radio stations, said they would help me out. After all, how difficult could it be?

I met with the students who ran the radio station at their weekly meeting and we introduced ourselves. They seemed to be a good group of students interested in music and I explained that I would be learning on the job from them. We seemed to get along fine. But when I tuned in the radio station on my car radio while driving home from work, I was so shocked by what I heard that I had to pull over to listen. It wasn't just the crude lyrics of the songs I found offensive but the comments from the disc jockeys, who attacked fellow students and teachers by name, discussed the physical attributes of female students' anatomies, and described their latest sexual and alcoholic adventures in detail. It was like three dozen young Howard Sterns competing to be the most offensive.

One of the first things I did was to contact some of my CMA colleagues and explain what was going on. They offered advice and e-mailed me copies of their rulebooks for student radio stations and condensed versions of Federal Communications Commission regulations regarding low wattage college stations. These were very helpful; at the next meeting with the students I handed out copies.

It became clear to me immediately that they had only a dim understanding of what was required of them in terms of eliminating profanity and slander and complying with the seemingly endless and complicated FCC regulations. We talked about public access files, prescreening of music before it was put on the playlist, and the legal limits on what they could say on the air.

At first, they seemed willing to go along with the new rules; we set up committees to deal with eliminating obscenity and to deal with all of the draconian FCC regulations about things like how long they had to stay on the air and all the various documents that had to be maintained, such as public access files. Within a few weeks, however, there was widespread rebellion. All of this was just too much work, they said. All they really wanted to do was play music on the radio. "This sounds like censorship," they said. "Why can't we do what we want?"

There really wasn't a choice, I explained. Failure to follow the rules could mean we'd have to deal with slander lawsuits from listeners and fines from the FCC. We could even lose our license. It all fell on deaf ears. It was much more fun to do it the way they had always done it, they said. The meeting ended with catcalls and raspberries. On the way home that night, I listened again and the station was back to the same offensive songs about the pleasures of raping women and disk jockeys describing in detail their personal exploits during their "fucked up" weekends. It seemed to me that they were deliberately broadcasting the most offensive songs and saying things that they now knew were slanderous and unprofessional.

Many of the station's listeners were local high school students and I could imagine their parents listening in. When I discussed this with the students, they told me I should stop listening to the station because it seemed to them that I was spying on them. I knew then that I was in way over my head and met with the student affairs administrators to ask for some help. They set up a meeting with the students and me to discuss the dispute and come up with a resolution.

I began the meeting by carefully explaining the situation and showed the group the FCC rules and the handbooks that were used by other colleges faced with the same issues. When it was their turn, the students complained that it was their radio station and that I was interfering with their right to do what they wanted.

Then I sat back and waited for the students to be read the riot act by the administrator in charge of student organizations. To my absolute astonishment, he said that the students were correct. It was their radio station, he said, financed by student fee money, and the college's policy was that faculty and administrators were not to interfere with their decisions. The students cheered as my jaw dropped in astonishment. I could not even speak for a moment.

What followed was a series of meetings at which the college's communication professors lined up on my side and the student affairs administrators lined up on the students' side. As an institution of higher learning, my colleagues said, our first responsibility was to teach students how to act responsibly and ethically. At the very least, students should be required to follow federal regulations. Howard Stern, we claimed, had no place within the academic community. The student affairs administrators were not moved and continued to maintain that students should be allowed to do what they wanted. These meetings reached all the way up to the vice presidential level, with the vice president of academic affairs agreeing with me and the vice president of student affairs backing the students. Because the two vice presidents had equal power, we were at an impasse and I resigned as the station's advisor rather than allow students to break federal regulations.

What I didn't know then was that the seemingly bizarre position of the student affairs administrators—that college students should be allowed to do whatever they wanted on campus—was the first of many encounters I'd have with what has come to be known as the "student empowerment" movement.

During the late 1990s, college administrators throughout the $600-billion-per-year higher education industry were beginning to reject the old model where colleges' primary mission was to educate students and teach them how to act ethically and responsibly. The new, modern ethos was to treat higher education as a business, where the students were the customers and the primary role of administrators was to keep them as happy as possible and to bend over backwards to ensure that unhappy students didn't transfer to a more student-friendly college that would try harder to satisfy their needs. Educating students, which used to be the primary role of colleges, became secondary to the new campus catchword: *retention*. Colleges that took a hard line against student misbehavior risked losing students to less rigorous colleges that had already adopted the "anything goes" philosophy. Colleges that refused to adopt this student-friendly attitude would lose students and soon go out of business, the theory went. Telling students things they didn't want to hear, setting high academic standards, and grading students fairly had all become secondary to the prime directive: retention.

During the next few years, I watched as this "retention at all costs" policy crept into the academic side of the college. The vice president of academic affairs who had defended me on the radio station issue was forced to resign and was replaced with a younger and much more hip administrator who listened carefully to what students wanted and gave it to them, even if it was not in the best interests of education.

In a public memo, he told students that plagiarizing information from the internet for their term papers could be defended as a trendy "mash up." At a college that used to value multi-culturalism, he dropped the foreign language requirement because students told him they didn't like it. He reduced the number of classes students were required to take to receive a diploma from forty to thirty.

Classes that used to earn three credits were magically transformed into four credits each and extended by a few minutes, even though the average student attention span was widely acknowledged to be only about twenty minutes. Students loved the guy.

But it didn't end there. The period of time that students had to drop a class was extended by several weeks, until the deadline was right before final exams. This pretty much eliminated the very unpopular practice of failing students who didn't show up or failed tests. Students could now simply withdraw from classes right before the final exams. And because students said it made them uncomfortable to ask their professor to sign the withdrawal form, my signature was no longer required. Students simply disappeared from my class and I didn't even know about it until I got my final grading sheet. And if, despite all these changes, students still weren't able to drop the class successfully, the student just got an "administrative withdrawal form" from an administrator.

This seemed like a curious practice, allowing students to drop a class rather than fail it, until a wiser and more knowledgeable professor explained it for me. Students who fail a class might get discouraged and leave, he said, but allowing a student to drop a class simply erased it from his record. Everything was set back to zero, except for one thing. The student still had to pay the tuition money for the class.

At about this time, I first heard the expression *super senior* for students who were in their fifth and sixth years at a four-year college. Many of these students had dropped dozens of classes over the years; therefore, they did not have enough credits to graduate at the end of their senior years. Other students were so poor at choosing classes that they had not signed up for courses that were required for graduation. This seemed like a crisis to me, but other professors explained it for me. Students who take six years to graduate from a four-year college, which is how long it takes at the average college these days, represent a financial benefit for the college, which receives 50 percent more tuition money for each student. "They want students to drop classes because it means they take in more money," he said.

The idea for this book dates back to that conversation and listening in faculty meetings as the new vice president of academic affairs praised the business model of higher education, which catered to its student customers, and criticized the old model, where education was the prime mission of higher education. That old-fashioned way of running a college, he said, was the "Mom and Pop store model," hopelessly outdated.

As I said, the students loved him, but many of my faculty colleagues began to whisper that the world as they had known it seemed to be coming to an end. Each year, freshmen arrived in our classrooms less prepared and more poorly educated than the year before. They were also much less engaged in the education process and less willing to work. Unlike the students of just a few years before, they seemed to have little interest in learning anything but were forthright in their demands that they be given high grades simply for showing up. It became clear to faculty that failing students was no longer an acceptable option. Increasingly, students refused to do homework, refused to read the textbook, and refused to participate in class, yet reacted angrily when they received a grade lower than an A.

In the late 1990s, it was still considered ethical to flunk students who failed tests, refused to do their work, and were not interested in learning. During the years from 2001 to 2005, however, these disengaged students gradually became a majority, increasing their power in the classroom and at the college. Professors who continued to post honest grades and refused to cave in to student demands were terrorized in their written, year-end evaluations by students. Administrators whose primary mission has shifted from education to retention were listening to those complaints and taking them seriously, fearful that unhappy students would move their digs and their tuition money to a more lenient college. It became clear to professors that their jobs depended on making students happy. That meant dumbed-down classes, easy assignments, little or no work, and high grades.

This was, of course, a major topic of discussion among the faculty, and I spent many hours over lunch and in the gym griping with them about it. Everyone understood what the problem was and why it was happening, but it was also understood that speaking about it at public meetings would be a career killer. Many of my colleagues' views ran completely counter to the "retention at any cost" ethic that the administration was spouting. Even professors with tenure knew that they would be punished for speaking out, so they remained silent. Professors who told me in private that "My students are so dumb I don't know how they find their way to classes" or "Of course I can't give her the grade she really deserves," simply refused to deal with the problem in public. The prevailing attitude was that the academic emperor's nakedness was not to be acknowledged publicly.

My colleagues from the national College Media Advisors, most of whom, like me, were former journalists, discussed by e-mail the phenomenon of colleges that no longer cared if students learned anything. Over drinks and dinners at national conventions in Washington, Kansas City, St. Louis, and Dallas, we agreed it was one of the great untold stories of the decade. Although little pieces of it appeared from time to time in stories about how illiterate college graduates were, the skyrocketing tuition rates, and grade inflation, no one had as yet strung all the parts of it together to deliver the inconvenient truth: most American college campuses had been transformed into something closer to adolescent resorts than institutions of higher learning.

By 2005, when I first watched John Merrow's groundbreaking PBS documentary *Declining by Degrees*, exposing the true conditions on college campuses, I had collected a cabinet full of notes, newspaper and journal articles, e-mails, and copied documents. I also tape-recorded and wrote down exchanges I had with students, administrators, and faculty at my college. I assigned my journalism students to look into some of the abuses. The students often had to use the Freedom of Information Act to gather information the college did not want made public.

I began to see how college administrators were misusing laws meant to protect students' privacy to cover up abuses that they didn't want the public, the press, or parents to know about. Despite the fact that my college was public and supported by taxpayer money, vast amounts of data were kept secret or, worse yet, deliberately distorted to protect the college's image and marketing position. Students who committed felonies like rape, assault, and arson were handled in secret campus judicial board hearings that were closed to everyone on campus. The results were never made public, despite my students' requests and Freedom of Information Act challenges. My college, like hundreds of other colleges around the country, was deliberately hiding its high crime rates and even lying on federal forms requiring full disclosure of campus crimes.

As my files grew, it began to appear that a large segment of the higher education industry was involved in a massive fraud in which parents, students, and taxpayers were being hoodwinked into paying for one thing—a college education—but were actually getting something entirely different—a five-year (or longer) party, where education was no longer required. It was a classic bait and switch. Parents were asked to pay tuition that increased each year at two to three times the rate of inflation, yet faculty salaries and spending for instruction remained constant. Most of the classes that freshmen and sophomores attended were not even taught by a full-time professor but by a part-time adjunct instructor, who was paid the minimum wage, didn't have an office, and wasn't invited to department meetings.

Where was all this tuition money going if not for education? The answer, I found, was that it was being used to pay for an ever-expanding number of administrative positions. Each year, colleges added assistant vice presidents, deputy deans, or directors for non-educational programs like graduation ceremonies, student activities, student nutrition, multi-culturalism, service learning, and student involvement. Salaries for administrators were also growing at an alarming rate. Some college presidents were paid over a half million dollars per year. The other main reason for the tuition hikes was the frenzy of campus construction, where colleges added multi-million dollar student centers, water parks, hot tubs, million-dollar workout centers, and climbing walls in a never-ceasing competition with other colleges to add the latest perk to attract more students. Even in the current recession, most college campuses are perpetual construction zones where there seem to be as many hard hats as baseball caps, and massive cranes and yellow construction markers are a permanent part of the landscape. Most of these buildings had no direct educational purpose but were designed to provide the frills that high school graduates looking for a place to party said they wanted.

When I discussed with parents what college classes were like today, they simply refused to believe it. How could college graduates be functionally illiterate? How could all that tuition money be wasted on administrative salaries and frills with little connection to instruction?

The idea for this book developed from those discussions with parents as I attempted to show how low higher education had fallen and how only one dollar in five of their tuition money was spent on instruction. Although many parents were aware of the term "party schools," for example, most seemed to have no idea how dangerous unsupervised binge drinking had become. Wikipedia defines a party school as a "college or university that has a reputation for heavy alcohol and drug use or a general culture of licentiousness." Estimates vary on how many party schools exist in America, but there are far more than the twenty listed on the *Princeton Review*'s annual list. But the problem reaches beyond the party school phenomenon to a related one that I call *subprime* colleges, where diplomas are being awarded to students who don't deserve them. Many of today's college students are not even aware that they are supposed to be learning things in college. For many of them, college is a simple cash-for-diploma transaction. They pay their tuition money and purchase a diploma. Education at these colleges is strictly optional. The 10 percent minority who want to learn are allowed to do so; the vast majority who are only there for the party get the same grades and are awarded the same diplomas.

Not all colleges and universities are party schools. Many of them still cling to the notion that education, not student entertainment, is their primary mission. And many students who attend party schools are still able to learn and resist the ubiquitous temptations to misbehave. But few colleges, from first-rate research universities to the Ivy League, remain untouched by the changes in educational priority I describe here.

I left my teaching position in 2007, right after the dean threatened to put me on probation unless I made my classes more student-friendly by removing grammar from my lesson plans and showing more movies. The administration had already expressed its frustrations with my concerns about the decline in the quality of teaching and my students' continued filing of Freedom of Information Act requests. Besides, I had a book I wanted to write—this one. I had a message that I thought parents and taxpayers needed to hear.

This book—written by a college faculty member who watched as his college was transformed into a party school and a subprime college, a parent, and a former education reporter of twenty years—is aimed at parents of college students and soon-to-be college students about what really goes on in many of today's colleges and universities and why. I will spell out in detail what's wrong with today's colleges, how it got that way, why it matters, and what can be done to restore the *higher* to higher education. It is my sincere belief that many parents are wasting tens of thousands of dollars sending their children to colleges where they will learn very little. These colleges award empty diplomas that many employers now understand are nearly worthless. By exposing these practices, I hope that I can be a part of the process of reform.

In these pages, I'll explain what you can do to make sure your children don't waste their college education money. I'll talk about the red flags to look for to determine whether your child's prospective colleges are more interested in keeping their students happy than in giving them the education they deserve.

I am a firm believer in higher education and what it can do for the bright children of America, but what is going on at hundreds of campuses today is not higher education or even lower education. It's not really education at all, just one big, non-stop party.

1

How Retention Replaced Education at America's Colleges

A generation ago, when parents sent their children to college, they knew what they were getting for their money. College was the magic doorway that opened up the American dream and those who passed through its gates could expect wealth, success, and a life full of meaningful engagement with the world. Students who survived the hard work and hours of serious study were welcomed into the ranks of society's leaders, both within their own communities and in national affairs. A bachelor's degree was the certificate that proved to the world that the bearer had mastered key skills, learned how to solve problems through critical thinking, and demonstrated the wisdom necessary to participate in the world of enlightened endeavors.

Because colleges accepted only the best and brightest students, just getting in the door was an accomplishment celebrated by parents and students alike as a milestone in their professional development. Those who gained admittance were already a part of the elite,

the leaders of tomorrow. The student who received a college accep-
tance letter had made the first cut for inclusion on the intellectual
all-star team.

The mission of colleges was clear. They were ascetic refuges
from the outside world, dedicated to knowledge and learning. They
were communities of scholars where free thought was encouraged
and young minds were nurtured and taught how to think. It was
a place where highly trained experts passed on the knowledge and
wisdom of the ages to a new generation. This mission had remained
essentially unchanged since the Middle Ages and its roots could be
traced back to ancient Greece.

Of course, there had always been students who got into trouble.
Many students were, after all, adolescents and prone to all kinds
of misbehavior, from swallowing goldfish and packing telephone
booths to all-night parties in the fraternity house. There were, however, limits to higher education's tolerance for misbehavior. Professors and administrators knew that an important part of their jobs
was to serve as the gatekeepers who weeded out the poor-perform-
ing and lazy students from the more serious majority. Students who
consistently scored poorly on exams, failed to read assignments,
or didn't bother to show up for class were eventually directed to
the college's exit door. It wasn't just a punishment for substandard performance; it was a way to ensure that high standards were
maintained so that the college degree would be awarded only to
those who earned it. This, in turn, guaranteed that the degree itself
retained its high value for those who did the hard work and demonstrated that they deserved it.

If you entered a college classroom a generation ago, you would
have found a professor at the front of the room lecturing or leading
a discussion about one of the important topics on the syllabus. Students participated or at least pretended to be interested in the topic.
There were questions that led to discussions, which led to a deeper
understanding. The vast majority of students understood that their
role in higher education was to take the time to prepare for their

classes by reading the assigned texts and coming to class ready to participate in the discussion. Studying was what students did and it was why they were there.

To ensure that the entire process worked smoothly, there were accreditation organizations that oversaw each step in the college education process, ensuring that standards were kept high and that colleges lived up to their primary mission: education.

Employers understood that a job applicant who held a bachelor's degree was guaranteed to be of higher intellectual quality than a high school graduate. Certified college graduates possessed not only a wide array of basic knowledge but the abilities to learn quickly, to make logical decisions when presented with problems, and to discuss matters in a sophisticated and intelligent fashion.

Today, unfortunately, almost everything you just read about colleges is no longer true.

The inconvenient truth is that only the best colleges in America still consider "education" to be their primary mission. Instead, since the early 1990s, colleges have been reinventing themselves using a business model, transforming themselves into Diplomas Inc., run by a new breed of college administrator more interested in retaining customers than in educating students. As a result of this change in focus, hundreds of college campuses have been deliberately transformed into havens of adolescent hedonism, where student misbehavior has become the norm and college administrators allow it because they don't want their student customers to take their tuition money somewhere else. In an all-out effort to attract and retain as many student customers as possible, administrators have given students exactly what they said they wanted: more parties and less education. Dining halls have been enlarged and reinvented as gourmet food courts and campuses have been tricked out with hot tubs, climbing walls, workout centers, water parks, and wide-screen television sets. Dormitories have been torn down and replaced with luxury condominiums.

The hard work that used to be required has been eliminated because students said they didn't want to do it. Don't want to read books? No problem! Reading them is no longer required. Grades too low? Forget it. We'll use a "grading curve" to transform your F magically into a B. Too busy to write a term paper? We'll waive the requirement for you! A new generation of students with a sense of entitlement demands Bs just for showing up and colleges, ever eager to keep their customers satisfied, are granting their demands.

Focused on increasing their revenue stream, today's party school colleges squeeze as many students as possible onto their campuses at the highest tuition they think they can get away with for the longest possible amount of time. To make their campuses more "student-friendly" and prevent their customers from dropping out or transferring to another campus, colleges have dumbed down their programs, sometimes to elementary school levels, and inflated grades so that nearly everyone gets an A or a B. Although there have always been student drinking parties, what has changed is that today the parties have become the main student activity at a major-ity of campuses, taking up far more time than attending classes or studying. Colleges used to be a place where students who were get-ting an education took some time off to drink; they are now places where students who came to party spend a few hours a week taking classes. A large percentage of party school students admit that they chose their college not because of its academic standing but because of its reputation as a party school, with minimal academic demands and maximum opportunities to enjoy themselves.

Party school administrators and faculty are aware of this decline in academic rigor but minimize its impact by calling themselves "non-elite" colleges and defend the decline in standards with the excuse that the unprepared and disengaged students that make up most of their student bodies probably would not have gone to college at all in previous generations. But is these students' college attendance really an improvement if schools dumb down their pro-grams and inflate grades to make students happy? And is it really worth tens of thousands of dollars to attend a college that is really nothing more than an adolescent resort?

Flunking out, which used to be the primary consequence for disengaged students who slacked off, has been nearly eliminated by party school administrators who think failing a student is a non-sensical rejection of a paying customer with cash in hand. These administrators have deliberately changed the priorities and rules of higher education to make it nearly impossible for students to fail. Professors are encouraged to make their classes student-friendly, and that means no outside reading assignments, no difficult concepts, no boring discussions, and no tests. Instead, they are encouraged to show movies, bring in guest speakers, and develop classroom presentations that are more "entertaining." Many of today's party school classes take their cues from reality television, quiz shows, stand-up comedy, video games, and three-ring circuses. They are long on fun but short on learning, but neither administrators nor students complain because both are happy. Students get diplomas without doing any work and administrators get to cash their ever-larger tuition checks.

Although colleges would still prefer that students actually learn something during their time in college, it's no longer required. Party schools have made education an optional activity. The small minority of students who are engaged in the education process and really want to learn something in college—about 10 percent according to the National Survey of Student Engagement—can still get an education as long as they avoid the temptations to misbehave that the majority of students constantly toss in their way. The majority of today's party school students take advantage of the "slacker tracks" through the curriculum, which allow them to obtain a diploma without reading a book, writing a term paper, or having a serious discussion. Professors are rewarded by the administration for keeping student grades high and keeping failures to a minimum under the official party school policy of retaining students at all costs. Today, 90 percent of college grades are either an A or B, where A is for the students who complete their work on time and B is for the lower half of the class who couldn't be bothered. All other grades are essentially off-limits because they discourage students and might tempt them to drop out. The minority of students who study hard in school and get a good education are awarded the same grades and the same diplomas as the students who did as little work as possible. So where is the incentive to study hard if the high-performing students end up with the same grades and same diploma as the slackers? In this way, party schools actually discourage student engagement in the education process. There is absolutely no reward for hard work.[1]

Party school policies also encourage students to stay in school longer than the four years that it is supposed to take to get a bachelor's degree. It now takes the average college student six years to complete a four-year program, adding a 50 percent surcharge to the advertised sticker price. Administrators make it easy for students to drop classes after they enroll, which means that students pay for a class without earning any academic credit. Colleges routinely fail to schedule classes that students require for graduation, forcing them to stick around for another semester or two. Students are permitted, even encouraged, to take less than a full load of classes. For students, that means more time to party; for administrators, who charge the same tuition no matter how many courses a student takes, it's an easy way to squeeze out a little bonus tuition money from their students.

With academic demands at a minimum, party school students have dozens of hours a week for what they call *socializing*, which is their code word for drinking themselves into oblivion. Studies show that nearly half of American college students abuse alcohol, but at party schools, binge drinkers make up a majority of the student body. Students whose self-abusive drinking habits were kept in check by parents and school officials when they were in high school arrive on campus at the beginning of freshman year to find that there is no longer any supervision at all. Arrests for public intoxication, public urination, assault, sexual abuse, and DUI begin the day the students move in and continue through the semester. Hundreds of party school students drink themselves to death each year. By the end of the first year, a quarter of the freshman class has dropped out, not for academic reasons, but because they simply could not remain healthy while regularly staying up all night and consuming massive amounts of alcohol.[2]

Party school administrators are, of course, well aware of this abusive pattern, but they claim their hands are tied because the students are legally adults and therefore free to make their own choices about how they spend their time. The reality, however, is that colleges that take a strong stand against student drinking by expelling repeat offenders or making their campuses alcohol-free find that their applications drop off significantly. Students looking for a place to party for six years are not likely to choose a college with a reputation for being tough on underage drinking. There are plenty of party schools around that deliver a different message to students: sign up here and you can have the time of your life.

The reason so few parents and taxpayers are aware of this dramatic deterioration in the quality and rigor of higher education is that most colleges have adopted strict confidentiality policies that deliberately take parents and the public out of the loop. Parents are prevented from talking with teachers, looking at their children's grades, or finding out what disciplinary actions their children have been involved in. Faculty members are instructed never to talk with parents, even if they call on the telephone or show up at the door. Party school administrators are fully aware that if enough parents and taxpayers found out what they were really getting for their tuition and tax money, they would soon be called to account.

The transformation of American colleges from rigorous academic institutions into party schools began in the early 1990s, when high schools began turning out a higher percentage of poorly prepared students unable to cope with the demands of college classes. With reading, writing, and mathematics skills in the elementary school range, these students were not able to read college textbooks, write term papers, or understand a college lecture. This created a schism within the academic community, with one side advocating dumbing down the curriculum to the incoming students' level to keep them in school and the other half demanding that rigorous standards be maintained, even if it meant a high percentage of students failed. This tended to break down along age lines, with the older professors defending academic standards and the younger ones advocating dumbing down the college.

It was at this crucial point that a new kind of administrator began taking over the reins of power at American colleges. These new administrators had more in common with Gordon Gekko than they did with Aristotle. They were armed with degrees in business administration rather than in education and had backgrounds or at least training in subjects like marketing, public relations, and management. These new administrators saw that the real problem with colleges was that they were not being run like what they really were—businesses.

To these new administrators, colleges were models of inefficiency because they refused to listen to the demands of their customers— the students—and were therefore always in danger of losing their market share to colleges that did a better job of customer relations. Money was being wasted on things students didn't care about—like libraries and seminars—and too little was being spent on things students said they really wanted—like hot tubs and wide-screen television sets. Colleges, they said, consistently made the wrong decisions for the wrong reasons. Why didn't colleges have balance sheets and profit and loss statements? Where were their plans for increasing their market share? Where were their customer surveys? Why weren't they targeting their markets better and giving their customers what they said they wanted, not what colleges thought they needed?

In the past, the prime mission of colleges was to ensure that students met high enough standards that they would *earn* a college degree. Now it was considered sufficient if the students *paid* for a college degree. The concept that students were supposed to learn something in college didn't fit into the business model.

At conferences all over the country, business coaches ran seminars for college administrators eager to adopt the new college-as-business model. This made the question of whether or not to dumb down the college moot. Colleges that refused to cater to the demands of their student customers would soon find themselves with a lot of empty classrooms. Colleges had to dumb down or die.

The takeover of American colleges by these new CEO-wannabe administrators with their eyes firmly focused on the bottom line completely changed the power structure of higher education. Faculty were among the big losers. In the past, teachers were more than just paid employees who punched the clock and collected their pay. Traditionally, professors shared in the administration of the college and had the power to oust a president who lost their confidence. Today, placated by jobs that require only a few hours of teaching per day, four months of paid vacation, and regular sabbaticals, most of the faculty have surrendered to the idea that academic standards must be lowered to accommodate students who sign up for the party and not for an education. That leaves faculty plenty of time to do what they really care about—their research.

The real problem with the new business model, however, comes from treating students like customers. A generation ago, students were thought of as powerless blank slates, the intellectual trainees who were required to meet the college's standards or wash out and be shown the door. Those who met the standards were granted a diploma that certified they had mastered the wisdom of the ages. Under the business model, however, students were rewarded with a diploma not for what they learned but because they paid their tuition bills on time. Under the business model, colleges moved dangerously close to becoming diploma marts where students did little more than purchase their certificates. A surprising number of my students voiced this exact attitude in discussions with me in my office. "I'm paying a lot of money to go here," they would say, "and I deserve a better grade than this!" For these entitled student customers, the old idea that you were supposed to *earn* a grade and a diploma by studying was an entirely foreign concept. For them, it was strictly a cash-for-certificate transaction and learning was not part of the deal.

Treating students like customers altered the campus power structure in other ways. A primary goal of the new party school administrators was to keep their student customers happy at all costs so they would continue to pay their sky-high tuition bills and not take their business to another college. Flunking students, no matter how poor their grades or behavior, became a bad business practice. Students who refused to read textbooks, who didn't show up for class very often, who failed tests and didn't participate in class, were allowed to get away with it over and over again. Students who drank themselves into unconsciousness, sold drugs, and even committed arson, rape, and assault were let off easy by college judicial boards so they could be retained as paying customers.

There was, in fact, only one mortal sin that could not be forgiven, one offense that would, without fail, cancel their invitation to the five-year party. That was failure to pay their tuition bills on time. Some of my best students told me they were about to be expelled because they had run out of money and didn't want to take out any more student loans. One student told me his name had been taken off the graduation list until he paid for a parking ticket. For these deadbeat students, there was no mercy. The administrators who had been so lenient and understanding about all kinds of other offenses became angry bill collectors, debt collectors who threatened termination if students failed to cough up the cash.

While the old school college administrators evaluated themselves on how successful their students became after graduation, party school administrators have become obsessed with a single number on the student's record: the bottom line. How much income does this student generate for us? They multiply the number of students at the college by the annual tuition rate times the number of years it takes them to graduate. This bottom line number could be improved by crowding in more students, raising the tuition rate, or keeping students in the system for more years. It should come as no surprise then that party school administrators have concentrated on raising all three of those numbers.

This may seem strange because most colleges are non-profit organizations and therefore unable to generate a true profit, but money is still power, no matter how you acquire it. Colleges with excess funds could give their administrators big pay raises, hire more administrators to lighten the load with many hands, and pay for non-stop construction projects designed to attract even more students. It was the winner-take-all strategy taught at business schools. More students—that is, more customers—meant more profit, which would enable the college to build more dormitories and dining halls to accommodate even more customers in a never-ending spiral of expansion. At the same time, excess revenue allowed party schools to add the kinds of expensive frills—like water parks and climbing walls, in some places—that they knew students were looking for.

Party schools call this competition to attract students the "arms race," where they rush to add the latest student-friendly frills to smash the competition in the same way that rival software companies seek the "killer app" that brings customers clamoring to their doors. Today, college promotional booklets referred to as "view books" are full of photos of students partying, students playing sports, students eating and playing in their dorm rooms. They resemble in many ways the brochures for luxury resorts or cruises. What's missing from them are photos of students in class, students reading books, or students studying. To even a casual observer of these materials, it's clear that the main attraction of a college education is no longer education. It's a five- or six-year cruise on the S.S. Party Barge and party schools do their best to deliver what they are advertising.

At the other end of the college process, party schools have flooded the job market with tens of thousands of semi-literate, unemployable graduates who aren't able to follow simple instructions. Even before the current recession, studies showed there were millions of graduates who weren't able to find suitable work and were forced to take positions as temporary office workers, clerks, pizza deliverers, and cab drivers. To make matters worse, these unemployable party school alumni were strapped with tens of thousands of dollars in college loans with payments averaging $400 a month. Many of these party school alumni now view their party school education as a kind of scam, promising them high-paying jobs but leaving them drowning in debt.

Meanwhile, party school administrators, following in the footsteps of the industry tycoons they seek to emulate, have increasingly been discovered with their hands in the cookie jar. College administrators have taken kickbacks from student loan companies for directing student business their way and sold the names and addresses of students to credit card companies to be targeted for marketing. Administrators were also found to have cozy relationships with the rich and powerful. "Clout lists" permitted the children of the well-connected to bypass the regular admission procedures. Administrators allowed students with the right political connections to obtain degrees without completing the course work. One study found that salaries for college administrators rose by a third in five years, and that doesn't include the generous perks that colleges provide for them, including $2 million homes, private jets, and golden parachute retirement packages.

All of this comes as no surprise to the academics who read professional journals such as the *Chronicle of Higher Education*, which has been publishing articles for more than a decade about dumbed-down classes, low academic standards, inflated grades, illiterate college graduates, the oversupply of graduates, and the antics of college administrators who wanted to emulate the lifestyle of Donald Trump. The mainstream news media doesn't exactly ignore the problems either. *Forbes* magazine, the *New York Times*, *BusinessWeek*, *U.S. News & World Report*, and the *Christian Science Monitor* have all run articles in recent years about what *Forbes* called "country club campuses."[3] There is no shortage of stories about skyrocketing tuition increases, the crippling debt and lack of jobs the party school graduates face, high crime rates on college campuses, and drunken parties involving hundreds of students that break out after major sporting events. There are also detailed profiles when a student dies of alcohol poisoning. What the national news media fails to report, however, is how all of these seemingly different kinds of college problem stories are really parts of one big story: colleges have been redesigned for partying rather than studying. And parents and taxpayers, the people who pick up the tab for the five-year party, never question the value of higher education, even when the price increases at three times the inflation rate.

In the following chapters, I'll explain how so many American colleges turned themselves into party schools and describe what goes on there from the point of view of an insider. I'll take you behind the scenes to show you how little education takes place in party school classrooms, how infrequently students study, and how their demand for dumbed-down classes and high grades has led to colleges where education has become optional. I'll also take you on a tour of college campuses showing you the dangerous levels of crime, including assault, rape, and arson, and how perpetrators are leniently prosecuted in the colleges' own secret court system. I'll explain how the dominant cult of alcohol consumption creates the last place in America where public intoxication is not only accepted but treated as normal behavior. I'll describe the steps that college public relations offices take to hide what really goes on there from the public, the press, and parents.

Finally, I'll show you how the low achievement levels of graduates and the high cost of party school tuition have financially damaged tens of thousands of party school graduates who are unable to find the highly paid jobs they were promised and are forced to make student loan payments of $400 a month for decades. In the final chapter, I'll outline the steps that parents and legislators can take to cancel the party school system. It's essential that we restore the rigor that American colleges need to train the leaders of tomorrow to compete with economic challenges from Asia in the coming decades.

Maximizing Profits at the Students' Expense

When party school administrators shifted their primary mission from educating students to maximizing profits in the 1990s, it worked because there was something in it for almost everyone. The dramatic increases in tuition turned administrators into powerful wheeler-dealers, academic Donald Trumps, who could design and construct multi-million-dollar campus buildings and increase their salaries. For faculty, the new dumbed-down classes and relaxed grading meant they no longer had to put much time and effort into preparing for their classes or grading papers. And the majority of party school students certainly weren't going to complain as their campuses were turned into amusement parks and class requirements for reading, writing, and studying were drastically reduced to make college more "student friendly" and where nearly everyone got an A or a B for hardly any work.

To maintain the party, however, it was absolutely necessary that parents, the press, accreditation organizations, and taxpayers be kept in the dark about the transformations that had taken place. Parents would likely raise a stink if they knew they were paying a higher and higher price for less and less education. Recent surveys, in fact, show that parents are beginning to doubt the value of higher education. Although just a few years ago, 97 percent of parents said sending their children to college was an absolute necessity for their futures,[4] a 2009 survey showed that the percentage of parents who believed this had fallen to just 55 percent. At the same time, the number of parents who had figured out that colleges care more about their bottom lines than they do about education has climbed steadily over the years to 60 percent in 2009. Only 35 percent of parents said they thought college administrators' prime mission was the education of students.[5]

Administrators know that colleges have a growing credibility problem, but many parents still cling to the old-fashioned idea that colleges will protect their children. Each time the news leaks out about illiterate college graduates, students drinking themselves to death, dumbed-down classes, inflated grades, the high campus crime rates, or how those millions of dollars in tuition money are being spent on frills, colleges have to turn up the propaganda machines to turn down the negative news coverage.

But that is only part of party schools' public relations problem. At the same time they try to turn down the coverage of student misbehavior in the mainstream media, they still have to make sure their potential customers, the high school students looking for a great place to party, are getting the opposite message: anyone, no matter how dumb, is invited to the twenty-four-hour party and no one cares if you learn anything or not. Why get a boring job when you can spend the next six years at our deluxe resort while your parents and the taxpayers pay the bill for you? You can have the time of your life without doing any work at all!

The ability of party school administrators to keep these two balls in the air at one time is a credit to their propaganda skills.

Although most parents don't realize it, they are the focus of a highly organized, misleading, and expensive public relations campaign beginning when their children are still in high school.

The Lies Told Along the Golden Walk

Party schools' public relations campaigns begin with what colleges call "the golden walk," when parents and their high-school-age children tour the campus before they make a decision about which college to attend. The walks are "golden" because they draw in the customers willing to pay the exorbitant tuition bills that finance party school operations. The tours are designed to seem casual and informal with a student walking backwards in front of the group, rattling off statistics, and engaging in supposedly lighthearted banter.

Don't believe it! The golden walk is the result of thousands of hours of careful preparation by college administrators and professional consulting companies that are paid thousands of dollars to make sure that what parents see is what party school administrators *want* them to see. The student tour guide's pitches are as carefully scripted as used car salesmen's spiels, thoroughly rehearsed and refined over many hours of practice.

Parents usually have no idea that when they take the "golden walk," they are not getting objective, honest information but a well-crafted sales pitch. Colleges know what parents are looking for and often engage in misrepresentation, misstatements, and even outright lies to entice them to sign up.

When parents ask admissions officers about the cost of attending the college, for example, they are shown the current one-year sticker price and told to multiply that by four, "with a little extra built in for inflation." This is the first of many lies and misleading statements that college admissions officers tell parents. Many colleges, like the one I worked at, state on their websites and their documents that they are "four-year liberal arts" colleges, even though it is well known that only 30 percent of students graduate in four years. National statistics show that 60 percent of students require at least six years to graduate. Parents will not find this very essential piece of information anywhere on college documents or websites. Lynn Olson, senior editor of *Education Week*, has referred to these additional college years and the costs associated with them as the dirty little secret of higher education.[6]

Parents usually don't learn about these hidden charges until their children bring home the news that they will need another year or two to graduate. These extra years in college are informally known as the "super senior" years and students refer to themselves as being on "the six-year plan." For parents who have attempted to budget for their children's education, these additional costs, which can add as much as 50 percent to the college bill, can be devastating. If they were somehow able to avoid taking out private student loans from predatory lenders up to this point, this is where they are finally forced to capitulate.[7]

Another stop on the golden walk is usually a dormitory room, which the tour guide might describe as "typical." The reality, however, is that the dormitory that parents are shown is the newest residence hall on campus with all the latest frills. These rooms, however, are usually reserved for seniors. What parents are never allowed to see are the freshman dorms, where students start their college careers. You can understand why colleges don't want parents anywhere near the graffiti-decorated hallways, broken furniture, and group bathrooms full of vomit and ramen noodles. At Keene State College, where I used to work, it was common practice to stack freshmen into these rooms like cordwood, with as many as four students assigned to a room designed for two. Why? So many freshmen leave the school during the first year—usually at least 25 percent—that colleges overstuff them in the fall to avoid having empty rooms in the spring.

Jeff Kallay, a self-described "experience evangelist" for a Pennsylvania-based company called TargetX, rents himself out to colleges at rates up to $20,000 to evaluate their golden walks. He said many college tours are led by "PR-spewing tour bots" who lack any connection with reality. Some of these guides are not above telling parents whoppers like "no one drinks here" and quote the "official" crime rates that everyone knows are artificially low. The just-for-show dorm rooms with their throw rugs and Green Day posters also send a phony message, he said.[8]

The underlying problem is that parents assume that party school administrators have their children's best interests in mind when they talk about whether their college is "the right fit" for their child. Parents still think that colleges put education at the top of their list of priorities because no one told them about the takeover by Diplomas Inc. The truth is that if your child is breathing and you have enough money to pay the bill, your child is always the right fit.

The *Atlantic Monthly* examined the college admissions process in 2005 and found that an entire new industry known as "enrollment management" has replaced what used to be the admissions office at many colleges across the country. The admissions officers are no longer college employees but work for private sector firms hired by the college to offer "image enhancement" and "strategic marketing position" in the battle against every other college to attract paying students.[9]

College administrators from the lowest assistant director to the president have been taught that they are part of a "higher education industry," where each department is a "revenue center," and students and parents are customers who must be lured to the market by a shiny new product and then retained by offering easy classes with high grades.

David R. Kirp, a professor of public policy at Berkeley, examined a number of college view books, the slick advertising brochures sent out by colleges to the parents of prospective students, and made an interesting observation. The books are full of photos of happy, diverse students, frolicking on the campus grounds, participating in sports, eating in the dining hall, or socializing in a residence hall suite. What is missing is any hint of what used to be the college's prime mission—education. Classroom shots are so rare as to be nearly nonexistent and there are few shots of students reading. Why? College officials know that most students don't want to be reminded that they are supposed to go to college to study, not to socialize. The books feature "pastoral retreats from the bustling world" but photos of students in classrooms are rare. "Only the bravest consultant is willing to emphasize the hard work of learning . . . for fear of scaring away prospective applicants," Kirp said.[10]

Given that they have been targeted with marketing material featuring food, frolicking, and fun that would not be out of place at a fashionable resort, it should be no surprise that students arrive on campus believing that they have purchased a ticket to a five-year party. It's one of the reasons students express dismay when professors demand that they read and learn something in their classes. That is not what they signed up for.

John Gardner, executive director of Brevard College's Policy Center on the First Year of College, said students begin to think of college as a continuous party even before they arrive because they are buying what the promotional brochures seem to be selling. "The overwhelming emphasis of a lot of that literature is 'if you come here, you're going to have the time of your life,'" he said. "It's not very common to have visiting students actually interact with faculty or sit in on classes."[11]

When the golden walks passed through the building where I worked, the brand-new Media Arts Center at Keene State College in New Hampshire, parents were impressed by the wide-screen television monitors in the lobby displaying student work or streaming live footage from the television studio. The parents lingered in the lobby for a minute, oohed and aahed in admiration, just as they were supposed to do, and then they moved on to the next station on the golden walk. When the walk was not in operation, however, those television monitors were usually not even turned on. What parents didn't see on their visits were the leaking roofs, backed-up sewers, and rodent infestations that had plagued this building since it had been converted from a defunct cafeteria.

If parents had visited my classroom just down the hall, they would have observed a much different and more truthful picture of what they could expect after their children were admitted. On a typical day, none of my twenty-two students would be taking notes and only a few would be paying attention. Two would be asleep with their heads down on the desks, three would be listening to their iPods or texting messages on their cell phones, four would be engaged in a lively conversation among themselves about the awesome party they went to last night. Some would be wearing their pajama bottoms, chewing gum, scratching their new tattoos or piercings, or eating their lunch. Only two or three students would have read the assignment for the day and they were the only ones who had a clue about what I was discussing. No one would ask a question and 90 percent of them were simply filling a seat, watching the clock, and waiting for the class to end so they could get on with their party school life.

Nips and Tucks for Tired Colleges

Most of the methods that colleges use to make themselves look good, like the trappings of the golden walk, aren't cheap—and it's the students and their parents who end up unwittingly paying the price. Party schools have rushed to change their official names from "college" to "university" during the past few years for no other reason than that a focus group told them it sounded more prestigious. Making such a name change may sound simple, but it costs hundreds of thousands of dollars to remake stationery, the college seal, signs, and even the carved rocks at college entrance gates. Of course, this kind of change is simply smoke and mirrors and has absolutely no impact on what is being taught. It is entirely a marketing scheme designed to gain a foot up on the competition. Focus groups and market surveys show that parents think *university* sounds more prestigious than *college* and that's all it takes for party school administrators to go into action to change their institutions' names.

Franklin Pierce College in New Hampshire became Franklin Pierce University in 2007 after alumni and public relations groups decided that the new name would be more impressive to employers and graduate schools. Previous graduates were invited to send back their out-of-date "college" diplomas for the more up-to-date "university" models. The same thing was going on farther north, where Plymouth State College was reinventing itself as Plymouth State University.

Beaver College in Glenside, Pennsylvania, which had been named after the county in which it was founded in 1853, faced a more drastic name problem, which led to a poor marketing position. In recent years, however, the college had taken an enrollment hit when the name became associated with something else. Hint: It wasn't a furry little animal that makes dams in ponds. To their horror, Beaver's administrators found that many high school internet filters, designed to block obscene websites, were not allowing students to look at the college's website. Any site with the word *beaver* in it had to be obscene.

Although Beaver College sweatshirts were popular all over the country for the same reason as Fairfield University's popular F.U. baseball caps were, the college's board of trustees hired consultant Dennis Nostrand in 1992 to reverse the college's sliding admissions and improve its image. Late night TV talk show pundits like Jay Leno and David Letterman put on their thinking caps and offered alternative names such as the "University of the Southern Region" and "Gynecollege."[12]

The college's marketing consultants, however, wanted something that started with the letter "A" so that it would be near the top on lists of colleges. Of course, it had to become a "university" as well. They eventually came up with Arcadia University, which the college felt sounded like a bucolic place for learning but which students probably associated with video arcades. In any case, the magic seems to have worked because enrollments increased by a third after the school's expensive facelift.

Another nip and tuck for college nameplates involved adding the word *The* in front of college names. In 2009, Florida State University began calling itself "*The* Florida State University," joining Johns Hopkins and Ohio State with the definite article prominently capitalized at the front of their names. Not long ago, colleges competed with each other in terms of academic excellence, but in the dog-eat-dog world of Diplomas Inc., academics spend hours discussing the pros and cons of this seemingly ridiculous name game. Party schools are terrified of falling behind the latest marketing trend.

Marketers and public relations experts also found that most college mottos were seriously uncool and out of date. The University of Idaho, for example, scrapped "From Here You Can Go Anywhere" for "No Fences," but no one liked that either, so they changed it again to "A Legacy of Leading," which tested better with focus groups. The cost of this motto-mania was $900,000, but who cares? Party school administrators can just jack up tuition again to cover the cost.[13]

Rob Frankel, whose website proclaims him to be "the best branding expert on the planet," said many colleges have bland, unmemorable mottos. Stanford's "The Wind of Freedom Blows" is a good example. "That slogan blows," he said in an interview. He didn't like Dartmouth's "The voice of one crying out in the wilderness" either because it sounds like failure. There is, in fact, an entire industry of college branding consultants offering their expensive services to colleges who think that a makeover will give them a leg up on the competition. It's easy to spend this kind of money when you can just jack up tuition a few more notches to cover the costs.[14]

The "Arms Race" to Add Campus Frills

Another major reason for the soaring tuition increases at party schools is the incredible, multi-million-dollar race to build the most eye-catching campus frills to attract students looking for the best party. Greg Winter, a reporter for the *New York Times*, went on an expedition in the fall of 2003 to take a close look at the state-of-the-art amusement park campuses that colleges were building to lure students. What he found reads like a shopping list for a higher education system that has lost its mind.[15]

At the University of Houston, he found a five-story climbing wall that he said looked like it was transported right out of Arches National Park. It was surrounded by boulders and palm trees to make it more attractive. "Everyone says it looks like a resort," Winter was told by Kathy Anzivino, director of campus recreation for the university. And that is exactly the idea, of course.

He found the largest Jacuzzi on the West Coast at Washington State University. It holds fifty-three people. Students at the University of Wisconsin at Oshkosh can get massages, pedicures, and manicures. Indiana University of Pennsylvania has room-sized golf simulators. Pennsylvania State University has a 200-gallon tropical ecosystem with newts and salamanders, as well as a 550-gallon salt-water aquarium. *The* Ohio State University is spending $140 million to build a 657,000-square-foot entertainment complex featuring kayaks and canoes, indoor batting cages, ropes courses, and a climbing wall that can accommodate fifty students. The University of Southern Mississippi is building a full-fledged water park, complete with water slides, a meandering river, and what they call a flat deck, a moving sheet of water that students can lie back on and stay cool while sunbathing.

The champion of all this craziness is currently High Point University in North Carolina, which features lobster and steak on its lunch menu and an ice cream truck that roams the campus to provide students with 500 varieties of free frozen treats. The residence halls have valet parking and concierge services where students can ask the resident clerk to pick up their dry cleaning or make dinner reservations.[16] The dining halls feature live music and wide-screen, high-definition television monitors. On their birthdays, students are greeted by name and provided with slices of birthday cake. All of this is coordinated by a computer, which also keeps track of students' favorite movies and brands of candy bars and sodas. Students can sign up for automated wake-up calls with the college president's voice urging them to have a nice day. Planned for the near future is a building informally called The Multiplex, which will feature a movie theater, a sports bar, and a steak house.[17]

Anyone who has walked around a party school campus over the past decade would find it hard to ignore the construction cranes, orange barrier fences, and hard-hatted construction workers that have become as common as the ubiquitous red plastic cups that students use for illegal drinking. Colleges that engage in this expensive and insane arms race, as most of them do, have become increasingly disconnected from the real world as they raise tuition over and over to pay their out-of-control construction costs. Parents who want to know why college tuition is rising so quickly really have to look no further. Turning campuses into adolescent theme parks does not come cheaply, especially when student trends change from year to year, and woe to the college that gets left behind. College administrators defend the excesses as absolutely necessary if they want to stay in business. Mitchel D. Livingston, vice president for student affairs at the University of Cincinnati, said students and their parents decide during the first fifteen minutes of the golden walk if they are in or out. "They want to be wowed," he said. "If we don't wow them they go somewhere else that has more wow."[18]

There is no sign that the building boom is declining, even during the current recession. And going forward, the cost crunch from the recession will fall more heavily on what Maurna Desmond in *Forbes* magazine calls "country club campuses," schools that drained their coffers to build luxury dormitories, spas, and top-of-the-line sports complexes. Party schools felt they had no choice but to out-build the other colleges in the neighborhood. "If a college decides we're not going to have fancy dorms or build a shiny new gym, students are not going to that college," said Sandy Baum, senior policy analyst at the College Board. "People are not choosing the lowest price college and that's a consumer issue, not a public policy problem."[19]

The basic underlying problem is that parents and students are choosing colleges using the wrong set of criteria. Party schools have increasingly opted out of the education industry and become part of the entertainment industry. The low levels of learning are merely a by-product of this change of emphasis. Are students attracted to these theme park campuses really interested in education or just in having a good time? Increasingly, it seems to be the latter.

High Salaries and Elaborate Perks for Party School Administrators

College administrations aren't just spending money on marketing. They also spend it on themselves. Colleges have bloated their payrolls with ever-increasing numbers of administrators and managers. In 1976, there were three non-faculty professional staff employees for every one hundred students. Today, that has doubled to six per one hundred students. In addition, for the past eleven years, college administrators have received pay raises higher than the inflation rate and, in the past five years, college presidents' salaries have increased by 37 percent.[20]

A generation ago, before colleges were taken over by Diplomas Inc., administrators made only slightly more than the faculty because the job was seen as little more than an extra duty on top of their teaching responsibilities. Many of them, in fact, hoped that they would return to teaching after their administrative tenure. But as party school administrators began to act less like professors and more like Wall Street tycoons, the mushrooming tuition rates made it easy to jack up administrative salaries. Although in the past it was common for colleges to provide their presidents with a free mansion, complete with servants, college presidents of the nineteenth century wouldn't have dreamed of asking for golf junkets, salaries in the middle six figures, their own Learjets, and golden parachute retirement packages valued in the millions of dollars.

In addition, administrative duties have become much easier as presidents hired more vice presidents, vice presidents added assistant vice presidents, and deans added assistant deans. National statistics about the number of administrative positions that have been added by colleges are hard to come by, but on the few campuses that have reported on this, the numbers are staggering. At the University of New Mexico, where a study was made as part of a dispute between the faculty and President David Schmidly, it was found that in the six years between 2002 and 2008, executive salaries had increased $4.1 million, or 71 percent.[21]

During the summer of 2009, the Raleigh, North Carolina, *News and Observer* found that the number of administrators at the University of North Carolina's seventeen campuses had increased 28 percent in five years from 1,269 to 1,623, an increase that the president, Erskine Bowles, called "an absolute embarrassment."[22]

Nationally, the number of nonfaculty college professionals rose 123 percent between 1976 and 1989, the last year for which there were numbers, according to a 1998 survey taken by Research Dialogues.[23]

University critic Cary Nelson said all of these new administrative jobs were being created with limited oversight, often without even a formal search, creating what he called "an opportunity for patronage if not a perk."[24]

Sociologist Arthur Levine explained how easy it was to create new layers of administration in colleges: "More admissions officers were hired to attract more students. More development staff were hired to raise more money. More student-affairs professionals were hired to reduce attrition. And more finance staff were hired to control spending."[25]

The *Chronicle of Higher Education*'s annual survey found that college presidents' salaries had risen 7.6 percent during the 2007–2008 school year to an average of $427,400. The number of presidents earning more than $700,000 increased to fifteen, from eight the previous year. The highest paid president in the country, E. Gordon Gee of Ohio State, was paid a total of $1,346,225, including a $310,000 bonus.[26]

The increase in college administrative costs attracted the attention of Charles E. Grassley, the top Republican on the Senate Finance Committee, who said he was concerned that, at a time when the country was in economic trouble and students were having trouble raising the money for colleges, presidents should be increasing their salaries. "In these hard economic times," he said, "apparently belt-tightening is for families and students, not university presidents."[27]

The new presidents have changed the power structure on campus as faculties and their senates, which used to wield considerable power, have been bypassed and replaced by a bureaucracy of managers and administrators who follow a corporate ladder model taken directly from big business. Faculty are increasingly left out of the loop and have less knowledge of what is happening on campus.

"As the managers come to know more, they assume they know what's best," said Cary Nelson. "The more financially ignorant faculty are, the less they can intervene intelligently and the more managers will want to keep them uninformed. Financial secrecy in the corporate university eviscerates any notion of shared governance."[28]

Although most parents and taxpayers remain unaware of how much of their tuition money is going directly into the pockets of party school administrators, there are signs that faculty members are finally rising up and threatening to revolt. The best example of this is at the University of New Mexico, where the faculty overwhelmingly passed a vote of no confidence against President David Schmidly and his top administrators, charging them with "diversion of instructional funds to pay excessive administrative compensation, as well as cronyism and other irregular hiring practices by the administration."

Schmidly has a compensation package worth $587,000. An anonymous whistleblower complained about cronyism in the hiring and promotion of twenty-one employees, including Brian Schmidly, the president's son. The faculty complained that funding for instruction increased by 19 percent while tuition increased 50 percent during the same time. "Where has the rest of the money gone?" asked Ursula Shepherd, associate professor of biology.[29]

Meanwhile, the corporate CEO lifestyles of some college presidents have come under attack by critics. In Tennessee, for example, one college president charged $1,500 to the college so he could take his wife to Barbados. Another spent $4,700 for expenses related to a football bowl game, including a pep rally and reception in Tampa. And a third spent $5,700 to take his wife to a commencement address he gave in Ethiopia.[30]

When the Tennessee Board of Regents prepared its annual report for the twenty-four campuses of the University of Tennessee, the total for presidential travel added up to $470,000, including the use of the university's own airplane. The annual audits were required after a previous president, John Shumaker, was found to have misused funds and used the plane for personal trips.[31] In many states, state university administrators are among the highest paid public officials—many making two or three times the salary of the governor and supervisors of state government departments.

Endless Tuition Hikes, and How Party Schools Get Away with Them

College administrations pay for all this—from the fancy facades on the golden walk and marketing research to their own high salaries—by jacking up tuition costs. Since 1980, college tuition has increased by 375 percent, far faster than the 127 percent increase in family income. Although the cost to educate students at public universities remained nearly constant from 1996 to 2006, tuition increases averaged 6.6 percent per year.[32] The party school industry has gotten away with raising prices at two or three times the inflation rate, year after year over the past two decades, with nary a complaint from parents and taxpayers, who seem happy to pick up the tab.

Parents are so convinced that a bachelor's degree is the magic key that opens the door to future success that they pay the outrageous admission price, despite the endless tuition hikes, hidden fees, and surcharges. They take out second mortgages, cash out their retirement plans, and go deeply into debt. For them, this is an emotional issue. They want the best for their children and are willing to make tremendous sacrifices to get the best for them. Neglecting to get their child into a top college seems like a form of child abuse. But for party schools, this unlimited demand for their product makes it easy to keep pushing up the price tag year after year.

The ability to raise tuition whenever they want to has encouraged colleges to be models of inefficiency. Where is the incentive to be frugal, cut costs, or weed out deadwood when you can simply raise the price to cover the cost of any projects you can dream up? Colleges can go on buying sprees whenever they want by simply increasing the price that their customers pay. No matter how steeply the costs rise, parents always manage to come up with the cash. What parents don't realize is that very little of that tuition money is being spent on instruction. Most of it is wasted on frills.

Only twenty-one cents of every tuition dollar goes towards instruction, according to Richard Vedder, an Ohio University professor and author of *Going Broke by Degree*. The kinds of exorbitant tuition hikes we have seen over the past fifteen years are simply not sustainable, he said. As universities have become less productive and less efficient, more of the tuition money is spent on frills like athletic programs, climbing walls, hot tubs, and gourmet food courts. When state legislatures increase support for public colleges, Vedder said, they rarely use the money to make cuts in tuition. Instead, they use it to "fund large salary increases, add staff members, and build more luxurious facilities."[33]

Vedder found that the additional funds were used to raise the salaries and fringe benefits of administrators, hire assistant administrators to lighten the load of administrators, finance public relations programs, support athletic teams, and build top-quality food courts, condominiums, student centers, and elaborately designed campus landmark buildings. They also use the additional money to sponsor community arts programs, build alumni centers, and sponsor free rock concerts. That means parents who send their children to party schools are therefore getting less and less education for a higher and higher price.[34] Economists think the college tuition bubble that has built up over the last fifteen years simply cannot expand any more without reaching a tipping point where parents will simply not be able to pay the price, even with the aid of cutthroat predatory lenders. They think the long buildup and sudden crash will echo the housing bubble, in which many thought the price of houses would increase forever. In the meantime, though, if parents complain that they don't have the money to pay the bill, party school administrators simply hand them the application forms for private loans.

The "Unholy Alliance" with Predatory Lenders

Just as this book was going to press, Congress significantly revised the federal student loan program to cut out the predatory banks that had been administering the zero-risk student loan program guaranteed by the federal government. Before that change, however, students were the victims of a scheme that left them seriously impoverished for years.

Robert Shireman, director of the Project on Student Debt, said more than two-thirds of students required loans to complete their studies and the average debt level at graduation had increased 63 percent from $9,250 in 1993 to $22,000 in 2007. "It has been too easy to just throw higher education's apparent need for more money on the backs of students," he said, especially when graduates are drowning in debt and unable to get high-paying jobs to pay them off.[35]

It would be bad enough if these loans had been fair and above-board. They were not. On March 15, 2007, New York Attorney General Andrew Cuomo called a news conference to announce the results of a month-long investigation of the cozy relationship between student loan companies and college administrators. The colleges, he said, were taking kickbacks from the lenders in return for placement on the colleges' "preferred lender" lists aimed at parents trying to find the best loan deals.

Students were victims in what Cuomo called an "unholy alliance" between colleges and the $85-billion-per-year student loan industry. Among the targets of his investigation were six of the leading lenders—SLM Corporation (Sallie Mae), Nelnet Inc., Education Finance Partners Inc., EduCap Inc., the College Board, and CIT Group Inc.—as well as more than one hundred colleges and universities that seemed to be in league with them to fleece students.

This "unholy alliance between banks and institutions of higher education . . . may often not be in the students' best interest," Cuomo said. "The financial arrangements between lenders and these schools are filled with the potential for conflicts of interest. In some cases they may break the law."[36]

Lenders paid kickbacks to schools based on the number of students who took out loans with them. Lenders footed the bill for all-expenses-paid trips for financial aid officers to posh resorts and exotic locations. Lenders purchased computer systems for the schools and even put college financial aid officers on their advisory boards to curry favor. Lenders set up funds and lines of credit for schools to use in exchange for putting the banks on their preferred lender list and for the colleges dropping out of the direct federal loan program, which was designed to provide low-interest loans to students.

In addition, colleges allowed lenders to set up call centers that directed calls from parents to the college about student aid directly to the lenders' call centers, where the people who answered the phone pretended to be college employees. They were actually salesmen from the loan companies. Why bother with the government loans and all those forms, parents were told, when the predatory lenders here can do all the work for you? Here's their number for you to call.

The lenders then completed the fleecing of parents by getting them to sign up for student loan money that went directly from the lenders to the colleges, with the parents getting stuck with the bill. The students who contacted the lenders on the colleges' preferred list were found to have paid higher interest and accepted less beneficial terms than if they had shopped around for the best deal, Cuomo said. Often, colleges neglected to tell parents and students about the federal direct student loan programs where the rates were much lower.[37]

Cuomo's announcement, which played on the front page of newspapers around the country, sent the nation into full denial. College administrators were crooks? Those tweed-encased, nerdy navel-gazers stealing money from their own students? Taking kickback money from shady moneylenders? How could this be? It was, for most Americans, the first look at the rot inside the ivory tower that Diplomas Inc. had created, the first hint that a new breed of robber baron college administrator was running wild in the groves of academe.

With the benefit of hindsight, it's possible to see that it was inevitable that as college administrators began to act like businessmen, they would adopt some of Wall Street's nastier habits. There was, in fact, little oversight over how colleges raised and spent their money. State legislators and the press were not paying attention. Accreditation groups were too focused on minutia about requirements for majors to see the bigger picture. With $85 billion per year flowing from banks directly to the colleges, it was perhaps only a matter of time before someone figured out how to divert some of it into their own personal pocketbooks.

The fallout from this scandal continues today as we are slowly finding out how devastating the combination of sky-high tuition and predatory lending has been to graduates and their parents, who were forced to make loan payments the size of a small mortgage for decades after graduation.

Since the scandal broke, author Alan Michael Collinge, himself a victim of the student loan scam, traced the problem back to its source in the early 1980s, when hundreds of small student loan providers began to combine into giant corporations. Sallie Mae, which started out as a government agency, became private and the nation's largest provider of student loans. Sallie Mae and other huge lenders made significant campaign contributions to members of the House Committee on Education. In return, legislators systematically removed the rules that protected students from exploitation by lenders. They quietly removed student loans from the Truth in Lending Act and the Fair Debt Collection and Practices Act. Then they changed the bankruptcy law so that student loans could never be forgiven, even if the student declared bankruptcy.[38]

With the protections removed, student loan companies were free to become loan sharks on a massive scale, setting up loans with high interest rates and oppressive terms that actually encouraged students to default on their loans, thereby imposing penalties and fees that could double or triple the amount the student owed. All of this helped set up the scam that Cuomo exposed, but as of this writing, in November 2009, Congress had still not replaced the regulations to protect students from predatory lenders.[39]

There were many interesting stories about the administrators caught by Cuomo. During the remainder of 2007, news continued to emerge from the investigation as Cuomo subpoenaed college and lending company records looking for deceptive or misleading practices. "The student loan industry is a very complex and confusing marketplace, and as students try to navigate its murky waters to get the best loan at the best terms, the last thing they need are sharks baiting them with glossy promotions and deceptive offers," Cuomo said in October. "Students should be wary of such marketing and not allow it to deflect them from careful consideration of the merits of a company's loan offering."[40]

He found, for example, that one loan company, American Student Loans Services, used an American eagle on its documents and pretended to be a federal agency. Sallie Mae went out of its way to hoodwink parents and students into thinking it was still a federal agency and not a for-profit company that actually competed with the federal loan program. Other companies, Cuomo said, were using "misleading and harmful tactics" in their marketing practices. But as Collinge pointed out later, "Students tend to sign nearly anything their universities put in front of them in order to get registered for class" and few have the luxury of hiring a lawyer to examine the applications. Students, unaware of the new cash-for-diploma mode of college administration, thought that the universities were on their side when they recommended lenders on their preferred lender lists. After graduation, when they were financially ruined by huge loan payments, it was too late to read the fine print.[41]

David Charlow, director of financial aid for Columbia University, was dismissed by the college in 2007 after documents released by Cuomo showed that he had sent letters to parents and alumni praising a student loan company, Student Loan Xpress, in which he had a personal financial interest. Ellen Frishberg, financial aid director at Johns Hopkins University, resigned after Cuomo found she had received $65,000 in consulting fees and tuition payments from Student Loan Xpress.

"While our investigation has uncovered many dirty secrets of the college loan industry," Cuomo said, "the stock and money that Student Loan Xpress funneled to Charlow and Frishberg were among the most flagrant. At times, it seems that Charlow and Frishberg were working more for Student Loan Xpress than for their universities."[42]

Charlow had been on leave since April when it was disclosed that he owned $100,000 or more in shares of Education Lending Group, the parent company of Student Loan Xpress. Immediately after receiving the stock, Cuomo said, Charlow had placed Student Loan Xpress on Columbia's list of preferred lenders. In a letter to parents in 2004, Charlow praised Student Loan Xpress and urged parents to refinance their student loans with the company. At the same time, he accepted tickets to rock concerts and sporting events from the company.

During the same week, Lawrence W. Burt, the financial aid director of the University of Texas at Austin, was fired after he was found to hold 1,500 shares of Student Loan Xpress and had placed the organization on the university's preferred list. Among the favors he had received from student loan lenders were annual luncheons for his staff, paid golf vacations, tickets to sporting events, and tequila.[43]

Colleges also sold to the loan companies the rights to use the college's colors, insignia, and mascot on their promotional materials so that they looked like they were coming from the colleges. "When lenders use deceptive techniques to advertise their loans, they are playing a dangerous game with the student's future," Cuomo said. "Student loan companies incorporate school insignia and colors into advertisements because they know students are more likely to trust a lender if its loan appears to be approved by the college. We cannot allow lenders to exploit this trust with deceptive, co-branded marketing. A student loan is a very serious financial commitment, and choosing the wrong loan can lead to devastating consequences."[44]

Among those caught with their hands in the cookie jar in 2007 were representatives of some of the top American universities, but it was clear that the practice was even more widespread than reported, affecting hundreds of schools across the nation. At my college, the preferred lending list was posted on the college's website but was removed only a few hours after one of my students, a reporter from the student newspaper, inquired about it.

Many observers of the scandal, however, including former Labor Secretary Robert Reich, thought that what Cuomo had exposed was only "the tip of the iceberg," and that many more colleges were involved in the scandal in many more complicated ways. "By 2000," wrote Collinge, "it became apparent that some schools had all but abandoned even the pretense of concern for students' financial well-being and were entering into agreements with lenders for the purpose of making additional money from students, over and above the loan income that was being paid to them for the cost of attendance."[45]

Eventually Cuomo and the lenders reached a settlement. The lenders adopted the College Loan Code of Conduct and paid $9.5 million to a fund dedicated to educating future college students about their loan choices. What the scandal left behind, however, was a handful of college student financial aid officers who were forced to resign and, of course, surrender what little was left of higher education's integrity. If Diplomas Inc. could rip off their own students for personal gain, why should parents trust them to care for their children for four to six years?

The U.S. Senate conducted its own investigation during the summer of 2007 and found that universities had been using their preferred lender lists as bargaining chips, selling them to whichever loan company offered them the best deal.[46]

Collinge, who feels that the depth of the loan scandal will probably never be known, points out that there are 1,412 colleges where 80 percent or more of the student loans came from one lender and that of these, 531 were found to have 100 percent of their loans from a single lender, which is, of course, the "preferred" lender, even if it is not official.

"The fact that so many institutions are funneling all, or nearly all, of their students toward a single lender is clear evidence that the students had, for all intents and purposes, no choice in their lenders," he said.[47]

The 2010 legislation was aimed at reforming most of these abuses. Federal student loans will now come directly from the government, bypassing the predatory banks, and the law will limit students' minimum payments to just ten percent of their incomes.

Pell grant increases mean students also won't have to take out as many loans. However, the law does nothing to hold down the rapidly increasing cost of college tuition, so students will still have to go deeply into debt in order to pay for higher education.

Selling Out to Credit Card Companies

At the same time the student loan scandal was being discussed in Congress in the fall of 2007, *BusinessWeek* published a three-part series on an entirely separate financial scandal in which party school administrators were selling the names and addresses of their students to credit card companies to be targeted for advertising.

"Nearly every major university in the country has a multi-million-dollar affinity relationship with a credit card company," wrote reporter Jessica Silver-Greenberg. "The deals can be worth nearly $20 million to a single university . . . and, in most cases, the worse the card terms are for students and alumni, the more profitable they are for the schools."[48]

Armed with the names and addresses of students provided by school administrators, credit card companies bombard students with marketing promotions, sometimes several per week in a relentless mailbox bomb. Also, for an additional fee, colleges allow credit card companies to set up tables in the student center where students hired as sales staff make $5 to $10 for each application a student fills out. In return for filling out the form, students get free T-shirts, pizza, Frisbees, or candy bars. Given that most students are habitually strapped for cash, the offer of instant money is a temptation few students find easy to resist, especially if the card comes with the university's logo or mascot on it. Thousands of students signed on the dotted line for a high interest rate and used the cards to buy beer and pizza and finance their spring break vacations in Cancun.

Tamara Draut, author of *Strapped*, said colleges referred to the students who worked at the tables as "credit card pushers" and they were taught to use some high-pressure sales tactics. They offered the cards just before spring break as a way to pay for exotic vacations and told students not to worry because it would be easy to pay back the money once they snared a high-paying job after graduation. About 25 percent of students use their credit cards to pay tuition, she said. "Visa and MasterCard have no doubt funded a great many pizzas, kegs, and spring breaks," she said, all at 23 percent interest.[49]

BusinessWeek found that the deals were bringing in big bucks from the credit card companies: $16.5 million at the University of Tennessee, $14 million at the University of Michigan, $14 million at Michigan State University, and $13 million at the University of Oklahoma.[50]

Although the colleges tend to shroud these agreements in secrecy, *BusinessWeek* was able to determine that the Bank of America alone had 900 of these affinity agreements with American colleges and Chase had an additional forty. They pay royalties to the colleges for the contract and a set fee for each student who signs up for a card. "Schools don't want the public to see money made on these deals and so they broker the contracts through incorporated entities," said Robert Manning, director of the Center for Consumer Financial Services at the Rochester Institute of Technology. "There is so much of this money unaccounted for."[51]

Irene Leech, an associate professor at Virginia Tech who bothered to read the fine print on the contract for a student credit card, was shocked at what she found. "Students assume that if the university has an affinity contract with a bank to offer a credit card, the university will surely look after them," she said. "But these contracts are really money makers for the school, and not about services to the students."[52] And students end up paying the price.

About 75 percent of college students have credit cards, up from 67 percent in 1998. Before that, most students did not have cards because federal law required parents to cosign the agreements. The bills can quickly reach staggering levels when the credit card companies offer lines of credit of up to $10,000 to someone who does not even have a job. If they miss a payment or two, the interest rates can shoot up to 30 percent or more. By graduation, the average student has racked up $3,000 to $5,000 in credit card debt.

The New Hampshire Higher Education Assistance Foundation found that many college graduates were falling behind in paying off their credit card debt. In a report called "Clothed, Fed and Over their Heads?" it was revealed that recent graduates were forced to choose between making the payments on their student loans or their credit cards. The average student was carrying $3,300 in credit card debt that would take eleven years to pay off at the minimum monthly payment. Students who were also paying off student loans were carrying an average credit card debt of $4,500.[53]

The delinquency rates show that students really don't consider the consequences of their credit card debt. The results can be low credit ratings that prevent graduates from renting an apartment or buying a home. The New Hampshire study found that 21 percent of college freshmen were at least four months behind in their payments and that 42 percent of students had at least six open credit cards.[54]

Consumer groups say that colleges, instead of pushing students into the hands of credit card companies, should ban them from campuses in the best interest of students. "The companies should not be targeting a population who are not in a position to handle credit wisely," said Travis Plunkett of the Consumer Federation of America.[55]

In February 2010, a new federal law went into effect protecting students from credit card abuses by their colleges. Students under the age of 21 are no longer permitted to apply for credit cards. Colleges are prohibited from peddling the cards on campus and anywhere near the campus and are no longer allowed to give out free gifts to applicants.[56] Thankfully, this is one way colleges won't be able to exploit their students in the future, unless they can find a loophole in the law.

Study Abroad Scams

Party school administrators don't need the assistance of student lending firms and credit card companies to fleece their students systematically. Even an innocuous-sounding program like "Study Abroad" provides ample opportunities to part students from their cash.

This scam first came to light when Jennifer Bombasaro-Brady, a student at Wheaton College in Massachusetts, returned from a study abroad semester in South Africa and complained that she had been forced to pay full tuition, room, and board at the Wheaton campus, even though she had not been there all semester. The program she attended in Africa actually cost $4,439 less than her Wheaton bill. "I was living in a place with no heat, no hot water, no electricity and no internet and paying the cost of my dorm room here," she said. Her father, attorney James Brady, filed a lawsuit in Massachusetts state court complaining that the college's pocketing of the difference in cost was a deceptive practice.[57]

Given that most countries in Europe and Australia provide much more assistance to higher education than the United States does, the tuition students pay there is significantly lower. So when an American college student studies aboard, the difference between American tuition and the foreign tuition can be significant. If the student had set up his or her own study abroad program, the student could have saved thousands of dollars. When they book these programs through the college, however, it's the college that gets to keep the difference. Some colleges even tack on an additional study abroad fee to pay for the costs of setting up the programs.

In January 2008, New York Attorney General Andrew Cuomo sent subpoenas to fifteen universities seeking data about how they determine the costs of study abroad programs and whether they receive cash bonuses, junkets, or other perks for steering students to particular programs. It turned out, he said, that there was a scam involved that was very similar to the student loan scam. Packagers of study abroad programs were handing out kickbacks, free trips, and other assorted goodies to administrators to sweeten the deals.

Wheaton spokesman Michael Graca said there was nothing illegal about what the college was doing. It charged all students the same price, he said, even though some courses were much more expensive than others. Everything evened out in the end. But at other colleges, such as Middlebury College, students pay the foreign colleges directly and the money does not go through the college, which can result in much lower costs.

When Brady offered to pay for the study abroad program for his daughter directly, he said, the college refused his offer and demanded that his daughter pay full tuition, room, and board even though she did not attend for that semester. If he tried to do it himself, he was told, the credits earned in South Africa would not be accepted towards graduation. "I think that's holding the credits hostage," Brady said.[58]

Cuomo said he became involved in the investigation because he was concerned that colleges had made improper "affiliation agreements" with study abroad packagers who marketed their programs to colleges. This came after a study abroad professional organization, the Association of International Educators, released a report listing "potentially questionable financial arrangements between colleges and program providers." Cuomo and an association of international educators later came up with a "code of conduct" to regulate the programs.[59]

Because they have not been informed that Diploma Inc. party school administrators have taken over, parents still cling to the outdated notion that colleges will protect their children and keep them safe during the nine months of the year they spend on campus. Nothing could be further from the truth. As this chapter has shown, college administrators are hoodwinking parents and systematically fleecing their children. They sell their students out to predatory lenders and credit card companies that leave students so deeply in debt that it takes them decades to recover.

At the same time, they employ high-pressure sales tactics, deceptive marketing, and elaborate public relations programs to convince parents to pay the exorbitant costs of college tuition. Only one tuition dollar in five is used for what parents think they are buying—instruction. In reality, parents are paying for the very programs and people who are cheating them. For party school administrators, parents are nothing but chumps who are paying higher and higher prices for less and less education.

How Education
Became Optional

he campus of Western Kentucky University, located sixty-five miles north of Nashville, sits on top of a hill overlooking the city of Bowling Green, so there's no mystery about why its sports teams are called the Hilltoppers. The college's sports mascot, Big Red, is a furry Muppet-like character who encourages fans at sporting events to wave red towels in recognition of E.A. Diddle, a semi-legendary former basketball coach. A former teachers' college, WKU offers eighty-eight academic majors to its seventeen thousand undergraduates, who pay $3,600 per semester in tuition. So in many ways it is a typical subprime college.

Among WKU's best teachers is Brian Strow, an assistant professor of economics who won the college's 2004–2005 Teacher of the Year Award. He's also a city commissioner, a former candidate for mayor, and an enthusiastic Chicago White Sox fan. He began his working career as a paperboy and has also spent time as a farmhand, a projectionist, and a phone-a-thon caller. He's married to another economics professor at the college. In other words, he is everything parents and students could want in a teacher.

Strow allowed a Public Broadcasting Service film crew into his classroom and the resulting footage was used in the 2005 documentary, *Declining by Degrees: Higher Education at Risk*, to demonstrate what goes on these days inside a typical college classroom.

Like most college professors at subprime colleges, Strow has to deal with students from a wide range of socioeconomic groups, academic abilities, and levels of engagement. A few students choose his "Introduction to Economics" class because they are interested in economics and want to learn more about it, but most of his students, he admits, are only interested in earning some credits to fulfill a graduation requirement. The vast majority of his students want to do as little work as possible. In that way, his class is typical of thousands of classes in party schools across the nation. Dealing with this wide variety of students in the same class can be a real challenge.

"I have students in that class who I'm confident would excel at any Ivy League college all the way down to students that I'm surprised they let out of high school," he said. He has had to dumb down his class extensively over the years to compensate for increasingly disengaged and poorly prepared students. The textbook, which used to be mandatory, is now optional. He tells his students that those who want to learn can buy it. Those who don't care if they learn anything or not can get by without it. Most of his assignments don't come from the book but from a magazine, *The Economist*. Even when his students were informed ahead of time that they would be featured in a PBS video, many of them arrived late and slept through his class. None of them asked questions or engaged in any form of discussion.[60]

At the end of each semester, Strow faces a dilemma. The best students, the ones who took the class because they were interested in economics and who took the time to read the textbook, score 94 or 96 on the tests, which is obviously an A. No problem there.

The slackers, however, the majority who didn't give a hoot about economics, didn't read the assignments, and didn't pay attention in class, scored only in the 40s and 50s, which you would think would be a solid F.

When Strow adds up the grades for assignments and exams, the average for all the students in the class is about 55 out of 100. If he used the raw numbers and the traditional grading standards, he would have to flunk more than half his class. But flunking large numbers of students is considered a bad business practice at America's party schools, where administrators are constantly chanting the "retention, retention" mantra and keeping students happy is more important than maintaining educational standards. Failure, the administrators insist, is no longer an option. It discourages students, makes them unhappy, and encourages them to drop out or transfer to another college.

Flunking a student sets up the professor for hours of angry confrontations with students who think they are entitled to at least a B just for showing up and who have learned that it's much easier to cut a deal with the professor for a good grade than to study and do well on the tests. Unhappy students can mercilessly savage professors on their year-end evaluations of them, setting up additional confrontations with administrators, which could put the professor's job on the line.

So, reluctantly, to make everyone happy and to keep the peace, Strow has invented a wonderful magic wand that he waves over his grade book to transform slackers into scholars. One wave of his wand and failing grades disappear and nearly everyone gets an A, a B, or a C. He calls it a "pretty big curve," a mathematical formula that adjusts students' grades significantly upward.

"A 40 magically becomes a C," he said. "It's retention, retention, retention that we focus on and for valid reasons. Most of our students are the first ones in their families to go to college."[61]

Gary Ransdell, the president at WKU, not only defends this blatant dumbing down of class content and grade inflation but insists upon it to keep the college's wheels turning efficiently. "The Commonwealth of Kentucky tells President Ransdell that your budget will be based on how many students you enroll, retain and graduate," he told his PBS interviewer. "If he (Strow) wants to get paid he's going to retain students. It does us no good and it does the Commonwealth of Kentucky no good for students to enroll and then leave."[62]

Randsell talks about enrollment, retention, and graduation but leaves out the word that used to be the most important mission of colleges and universities: education. The justification for the dumbing down of America's party schools only works if you conveniently forget that education is the reason colleges exist in the first place. If you leave education out, the whole process becomes a simple exercise in certificate purchasing. Students pay tuition to buy the diploma that the college is selling. You can learn something if you want, but if you'd rather not bother, that's okay. They'll sell you a diploma anyway.

Cooking your grade book to give students passing grades they do not deserve is so common at party schools these days that faculty and administrators don't even think twice about doing it. The practice, as Strow says, is so essential to the operation of colleges in the twenty-first century that they simply could not function without it. Without grade inflation and dumbing down of classes, many colleges would be facing nearly empty classrooms and professors would have to be laid off. When a college's retention policy conflicts with maintaining academic standards, as they do in Strow's classroom, academic standards lose every time. Strow's students' raw grades show that most of them don't know very much about economics, but Strow's legerdemain grading formula pretends that they do. Although his students' transcripts say they passed "Introduction to Economics," the reality is that most of them didn't really learn very much and are nearly as ignorant of economics as when they entered his class.

What happens in Strow's class is repeated in tens of thousands of classrooms in hundreds of party schools throughout America. I have spoken to more than a hundred professors who have faced exactly the same dilemma: do you give the students the grades they really deserve and thereby anger your bosses and sentence yourself to hours of confrontations or do you simply make a few adjustments to ensure that students and administrators are happy?

While there are still a few holdouts who cling to the out-of-fashion idea that students who refuse to learn should fail, the vast majority of professors choose to give the students what they want. Strow's grading curve is only one of the ways this works. Sometimes students who failed the tests and blew off assignments are awarded "extra credit" by generous professors. More commonly, the entire class is simply dumbed down to elementary school levels from the start so that every student can pass the tests without studying or even reading the textbook.

When I asked professors how they could justify this, many of them replied, as Strow did, that given that these students are the first ones in their families to go to college, professors need to cut them some slack. But this argument only makes sense if you believe that going to college in and of itself carries some kind of benefit, even if you don't do any work, read any books, or pay attention in class. It seems to imply that knowledge can be absorbed by students from the college atmosphere.

What is actually taking place is a form of widespread fraud: certifying that students have learned something that they have not learned. If you probe deeper, professors who advocate this kind of grade inflation see it as a form of social engineering to increase the number of college graduates and hopefully increase their earning potential. Eventually, party schools grant diplomas to students who have not learned anything approaching what used to be required of them.

This widespread fraud allows party schools to collect the tuition money that keeps the wheels of Diplomas Inc. happily turning and avoids angry confrontations with its student customers. Everyone gets to go home happy by pretending that those high grades really mean the students learned something.

A generation ago, students who refused to read assignments and earned a score of 40 on the tests would have received the grade they really deserved: an F. Eventually, they would have flunked out. But in the twenty-first century, thanks to the influence of the new breed of CEO-wannabe party school administrators, higher education is less interested in education and more interested in keeping students happily paying their tuition bills, which increases their revenues. Failing students, no matter how little they have learned or how little effort they are making, is considered a poor business practice. After all, why drive paying customers away? Why ruin these students' future by flunking them out of college?

Over the past decade, classes have been dumbed down and then dumbed down again to eliminate difficult concepts, reduce the amount of required reading and writing, and reduce the amount of critical thinking skills that students need to become the leaders of tomorrow. When students still aren't able to learn it, despite the reduced expectations, they are simply given inflated grades that they did not earn. Today's college students are aware that there is an alternative path to a passing grade. They can study hard, as a minority of them do, or they can show up in the professor's office the last week of classes and negotiate a deal for a grade. So many students show up during this last week of classes to request grade manipulation that it has come to be known as *slacker week*. Students know that professors cannot flunk very many students because it is no longer considered acceptable by the administration. They know that colleges consider them valuable customers in the debt-for-diploma exchange. Students want a diploma and they are willing to pay for it, but for most of them, reading, writing, and studying are not part of the deal. Only chumps waste time studying for exams or reading the textbook when they can get a B just for showing up. To Strow and Ransdell, this system of awarding passing grades to students who should have flunked out seems like a genuine win-win situation for everyone involved. The students are awarded their diplomas without doing much work and the college gets to keep the money from tuition and state aid to pay their salaries and keep the process running.

But it's not a winning situation for everyone. What about the parents who saved all their lives and went deeply into debt to pay for a college education for their children? Do parents think they are purchasing a diploma or do they think they are buying an education? What about taxpayers who are helping to support these new learning-optional college campuses? What about employers looking for educated job applicants who are confronted with degree holders who can't read?

The problem is that under the new business model adopted by party school administrators, obtaining a diploma is no longer the same as earning one. Anyone who can follow a few simple rules and keep their tuition bills paid can purchase a diploma. Many of America's colleges, particularly at the third and fourth tiers, are really not in the education business any more but have become diploma marts where students purchase the credentials they want without having to do the work that used to be required to earn them. Most parents I spoke with had no idea that this significant erosion of academic standards had taken place. They still believed, often falsely, that higher education was taking place in colleges. Many of them told me that they simply could not believe the inconvenient truth that colleges were no longer performing the task they were designed to do. Although the price tag soars more and more every year, academic standards have dropped to elementary school levels. Party schools get away with this because parents, the public, and the press aren't really paying attention.

If we take a closer look at this process, it begins to resemble a massive scam that damages students, the educational system, and even the nation, which depends on colleges to educate our future leaders. Awarding students grades they do not deserve for work they did not perform, which pleases students in the short term, severely shortchanges them in the long run by giving them false feedback about their abilities, skills, and levels of knowledge. It also leaves a very large gap between the body of knowledge that society expects students to acquire in college and the low level of learning that is really taking place.

While a few college students still take their education seriously and choose courses based on what they will need to know after graduation, it's easy for students to find the slacker tracks through college. Students know which courses are easy and which courses are taught by easy grading professors and share this information with each other on websites like ratemyprofessors.com. Colleges allow students to choose classes based on a kind of Chinese menu system. Students choose a class from column A and another from column B until they obtain enough credits in all the categories of requirements. In some cases, these classes might result in a fairly balanced education, but in most cases it leaves large holes in their body of knowledge.

Most colleges, in fact, have no idea what kinds of knowledge students have acquired during those four to six years because they don't administer some of the widely available exams that were designed by organizations like the College Board to show exactly how much knowledge was acquired between freshman year and graduation. Colleges claim that this test would simply add an additional burden on students and faculty, but the real reason is that party school administrators don't want the world to know how little knowledge graduates have obtained, even in their majors, about things like history, writing, geography, the arts, economics, civics, science, and math. When outside groups administer similar tests, the low level of student learning makes headlines. The results show that college seniors can't read well enough to understand a newspaper editorial or a simple chart. They can't solve fourth-grade math problems involving long division. They don't know in which century the Civil War took place and can't locate the United States on a map of the world.

"American higher education has lost its bearings and is falling short in its vital educational mission," said one national expert. "I believe our system has developed serious flaws that interfere with its ability to develop in our young people the depth of critical thinking, intellectual curiosity, and human understanding so essential to dealing with the problems in our world today."[63]

Dumbed-Down Classes

Because the majority of students at party schools refuse to do the hard work that used to be required in college, colleges have been forced to dumb down their classes to the level that underperforming students can handle. The lower the standards, the more students will meet the mark without all the bother of making any effort to study or learn. Many professors, however, are complaining that the process has reached ridiculous levels.

Paul Sally, a math professor at the University of Chicago, for example, said graduating "numerically illiterate" students was creating an entire generation that doesn't know how to balance a checkbook. "This is a serious, serious problem," he told a meeting of the Mathematical Association of America in 2003. "You can't teach mathematics with cotton candy." He found that colleges across the country have replaced courses that actually used to teach students how to *do* math with courses *about* math.[64]

"They are describing what is going on in mathematics without demanding any of the skills it takes to do it and without telling them what mathematics means," he said. Concepts considered too difficult for students are left out entirely. Students call these dumbed-down classes "Math for Rocks" or "Math for Dummies," he said. They feature "beautiful pictures and imprecise ideas. . . . It's like learning to drive a car by watching a video and then being told to go drive on the expressway."

Creating classes that are easy for students to pass without doing any hard work is cheating them in the long run, he said. Students who lack basic math skills have trouble following the stock market or understanding medical studies, getting a mortgage, balancing their checkbooks, or doing their taxes.

In the Department of Communication at Keene State College, where I was employed for a dozen years, all students were required to take a capstone course called "Senior Project" in their senior year. Students constantly told me how difficult this class was, how much time it took, and the large amount of work involved. I never taught this dreaded course, but when I looked at the syllabus, I was amazed to find that students were required to do only one thing during the entire semester: write a single term paper. This activity used to be required as part of most college courses and was something high school students were once required to do. Now, after fifteen years of education, many of them were writing a term paper for the first time and taking a whole semester to do it.

The students met individually with an assigned faculty member once a week for each step of the process. It turned out to be a severe case of spoon-feeding in which the professor directed each stage of the process. There was a class for choosing a topic, a class for choosing sources, a class for researching the topic, a class on how to take books out of the library, a class on citing sources, a class on organization, and a class on proofreading. Students had their hands held during every stage of the process to the point that the final paper could be considered as much the teacher's work as the student's.

Given the amount of time involved, one might assume that these papers would be top-notch efforts. When they were presented at the end of the semester, however, some of the topics ranged from Paris Hilton and Britney Spears to the drinking habits of underage students to the role fraternities and sororities play in campus social life. I was often embarrassed to be a part of this poor excuse for learning.

An increasing number of professors don't even bother assigning term papers anymore because the students simply refuse to complete them. They don't have the necessary skills and are not willing to take the time to do the research and the writing. Their language and thinking skills are too poor and they don't have enough familiarity with essays to write one. They don't know how to use source information and they have a hard time focusing on one thing for very long. "In the old technique of assigning an essay, the student would pick the topic and they would go to the library and research it to determine if it's a topic you can actually write something about," said one professor. "Now, most students can't pick a topic. If you tell them what to do—okay, here's a selection of topics, pick one—they can do it, but on their own most cannot come up with a topic that they can write meaningfully about."[65]

Meanwhile, students have become bolder about voicing their objections to how classes are run. They interrupt lectures by asking, "Is this going to be on the test?" and they answer questions from teachers with comments like, "Who gives a shit?" When professors ask students to pay attention, they tell them to shut up and mind their own business because they pay their salaries. When I attempted to show a student how to make subjects and verbs agree in his news story, he told me to stop forcing my opinions on him and let him do it his own way. In another class, most of the students simply marched out in protest when they thought I was giving them too much homework.

Mike Flatt, the managing editor of *The Spectrum* student newspaper at SUNY Buffalo, explained student entitlement in a column. "Students today feel they have the right to walk in late to class and not be called on it," he wrote. "A student who works full time to pay for college shouldn't have to worry about showing up five minutes late . . . *I pay your salary. Who are you to lecture me on any subject (other than the class topic)?* A tenuous power struggle takes place between students and professors, and some professors seem to be missing the bigger picture. We, as students, as paying clients, deserve to send the message to an instructor if we don't believe they're giving us an adequate return on our investment. And mocking students for punctuality is poor customer service."[66]

In other words, the old dynamic in which the professor was in control of the class, set the standards, and acted as gatekeeper in deciding which students had mastered the information and were ready to move on, has been turned upside down. Now it is the students who set the standards and they can get really angry if they feel the standards are too high. Professors who have problems with the new rules can expect to be out of a job.

The Professor as Entertainer

In countless written evaluations of faculty, students repeat the same complaints over and over. Classes are boring. Professors aren't entertaining enough, not funny enough. "Bring a pillow," students sometimes write, or "He needs some dancing girls or a monkey or something to make his class more interesting." To meet these demands, professors take acting classes and train themselves to be more demonstrative. They search the internet for some new jokes to use in their classes. The goal is to turn their classrooms into stand-up comedy clubs, circuses, or television variety shows.

To see where all of this is heading, you can take a look at the popular HBO comedy series *Assume the Position with Mr. Wuhl*, which uses a college classroom for a setting. It's not real, of course, but it is everything students could want: fast-paced action with lots of explosive sounds, scantily clad models, rapid-fire changes of topic and format. For students, it's a laugh-a-second romp through such topics as why President William Henry Harrison died of pneumonia, whether or not cupcake icon Little Debbie really existed, and a PowerPoint reenactment of the death of Alexander Hamilton, complete with pistol graphics and sound effects.

Entertaining? Unquestionably. But educational? Well, not really. This kind of approach, which is imitated by countless professors eager for the elusive thumbs-up on student evaluations, is aimed at getting a quick laugh or making an interesting but trivial point. It's college without all that complicated critical thinking. Students can sit back and enjoy the show until the class ends. But education as scripted by Mr. Wuhl is nothing but a collection of Trivial Pursuit cards without any connections, critical thinking, or any real knowledge being added. It's what children who grew up watching *Sesame Street* expect from education: lots of short little vignettes with lots of colors and sounds, none of it requiring any real thinking.

Tom Fleming, one of the most popular teachers at Arizona State University, has turned his "Introduction to Astronomy" class into a high-tech quiz show. His classroom is equipped with portable feedback devices called "classroom clickers" that students use to choose among four options at critical points in his lectures. Students express their opinions by pushing one of four buttons and the total results are registered on the screen at the front of the class.

"I can sit here and rant and rave that our standards are low and our students don't learn in high school what they used to, but the fact of the matter is that I have 135 students here and now and I can't go back and change history about what kind of high school education they received," he said. "They're here. They're paying their tuition money and as I tell them on the first day of class, I'm going to give you your money's worth."[67]

Almost none of the students who take his class are astronomy majors or even science majors but art students, business majors, and journalists, who require nine credits in science to fulfill a graduation requirement.

To fellow teachers who complain that he is doing nothing more than "putting a happy face" on education or turning his class into a circus, he replies that he is using what he calls the "Mary Poppins" principle: "A spoonful of sugar does help the medicine go down."

Derek Bruff, assistant director of the Center for Teaching at Vanderbilt, has written an entire book for college teachers about innovative ways to use classroom clickers or "Classroom Response Systems," as they are officially called. Students who are afraid to raise their hands in class, he said, find it less intimidating to push a button and have their response recorded electronically. If this sounds suspiciously like *Who Wants to Be a Millionaire?*, that's the idea, only there are no lifelines that let students call their mothers if they get stumped. These classes are, of course, very popular with students, but many professors worry, with good reason, that as clickers replace the traditional lectures and seminars on college campuses, critical thinking has taken a giant step backwards.[68]

Walter H. G. Lewin, a seventy-one-year-old physics professor at MIT, has turned himself into an internet star by using costumes and props in his classes. Videos of his classes are stored on the internet and watched by thousands of viewers who never set foot in his classroom. He also has found a way to become a kind of circus performer to illustrate the laws of physics. He beats a student with cat fur to demonstrate electrostatics. Wearing shorts, sandals with socks, and a pith helmet, he fires a cannon loaded with golf balls at a stuffed monkey wearing a bulletproof vest to demonstrate the trajectories of objects in free fall. He rides a fire-extinguisher-propelled tricycle across the room to show how a rocket works.[69]

Not only is he popular with his students, his videos are among the most popular on YouTube, and he receives a constant barrage of fan mail from both college and high school students around the country.

To demonstrate how a pendulum works, he hangs an iron ball from the ceiling on a long rope. The ball swings back and forth but stops just short of his chin. "Physics works," he proclaims. He told the New York Times that he spends twenty-five hours preparing each of his lectures, choreographing each detail, and paring the information down to the essential parts. Anything boring is discarded. Fun and clarity are the important elements. For many students all over the country, this is the ideal teacher and the ideal class.

Another professor who has made it into the ranks of celebrity is Paul Worsey of Missouri University of Science and Technology, who calls himself "the mad professor" but who students call "professor pyro." In an age when motion pictures are rated by the number of car crashes they contain, Worsey is famous for blowing things up. He victimizes everything from tree stumps to watermelons to his students' favorite: textbooks. His class is being picked up nationally by the Discovery Channel. "I'm a little bit insane, so that helps a bit," he said during a television interview. "I'm the last person you'd call boring."[70]

Grade Inflation

Stuart Rojstaczer, a former geophysics professor from Duke, is the nation's foremost expert on grade inflation. He left academia in 2005 after writing a memoir, *Gone for Good*, about the decline of standards in colleges once the business model administrators came in and took over.

"Teaching is often more about babysitting and joke telling than it is about education," he said. "I like to tell jokes. Babysitting twenty-one-year-olds is another story. I had a working body and brain fully capable of doing something new. . . . I feel that higher education has lost its way. The quality of undergraduate education has seriously degraded. But no one seems to mind. In fact, parents and students seem to be ecstatic that we've replaced content with entertainment. They love our 'college as summer camp' model."

Rojstaczer maintains a grade inflation website where he keeps track of recent studies. In a recent op-ed piece, he described how grade inflation worked at Duke, which is generally not considered a party school. Each semester his grade report included only As and Bs with no Ds or Fs. He had not given a C in over two years. He has since collected data from more than eighty schools, all of which show grade inflation.

"The C, once commonly accepted, is now the equivalent of the mark of Cain on a college transcript," he said. How rare has the C become? His data indicates that "not only is C an endangered species but . . . B, once the most popular grade at universities and colleges, has been supplanted by the former symbol of perfection, the A."[71]

Even non-subprime colleges show signs of this same grade inflation. At Duke, fewer than 10 percent of grades are Cs, a significant decline since 1969, when a quarter of the grades awarded were

Cs. The A supplanted the B as the most popular grade in the early 1990s. At Pomona College, less than 4 percent of grades are Cs. Approximately 50 percent of all grades at Duke, Pomona, Harvard, and Columbia are As, while Ds and Fs represent just 2 percent of all grades given. Grade point averages among colleges that publish this data are rising at the rate of about 0.15 points every decade, Rojstaczer found.

"If things go on at that rate, practically everyone on campus will be getting all As before mid-century, except for the occasional self-destructive student who doesn't hand in assignments or take exams—if exams are even given."

Grade inflation is a logical result of the changes that have occurred in the power structure at colleges and universities as the business model replaced education with retention. High grades have become an essential ingredient in the potent academic brew prepared by colleges to keep the customers satisfied.

"As are [as] common as dirt in universities nowadays because it's almost impossible for a professor to grade honestly," he said. "If I sprinkle my classroom with the Cs some students deserve, my class will suffer from declining enrollments in future years. In the marketplace mentality of higher education, low enrollments are taken as a sign of poor quality instruction. I don't have any interest in being known as a failure."[72]

Parents and students, the people who pay the tuition that keep the college in business, want high grades and professors are expected to cater to their desires.

Administrators are well aware of grade inflation but have come up with some lame excuses for it, Rojstaczer said. They say that college is teaching more effectively or that students are smarter than they used to be, even though the statistics do not back that up. "Many students and parents believe these explanations," he said. "They accept the false flattery as the real thing.

"Today's classes, as a result, suffer from high absenteeism and a low level of student participation. In absence of fair grading, our success in providing this country with a truly educated public is diminished. The implications of such failure for a free society are tremendous."

Alicia C. Shepard, a journalism teacher at American University, recounted how she was relentlessly pursued for weeks by students who received anything other than an A in her classes. They asked to retake tests and rewrite papers. They sent her e-mails. They showed up at her office demanding that she reread their papers. Thinking that this was somehow unusual, she asked her colleagues about her experiences and found the same thing. She was told about students who had slept through the midterm exam and showed up late for the final and then harassed the teacher who gave them a C minus.[73]

Arthur Levine, president of Columbia University Teacher's College and an authority on grading, told Shepard that many students who have come to see college as a financial transaction where they exchange cash for a diploma think anything less than an A means they are not getting their money's worth.

Students who are given Cs often react aggressively or passive-aggressively because they had been told in high school that they were outstanding rather than just average. They insist that they worked hard on the project in question, but the reality is that they worked hard only the night before for a project that was supposed to involve thinking, researching, intensive study, and several weeks of preparation.

Professors who go against the trend of providing easier courses and higher grades can face severe consequences, from being viewed as "dinosaurs" or "out of touch" by their hipper colleagues to unpleasant encounters with students. Professors have to deal with seasoned grade-mongers who pester them incessantly, sometimes resorting to objectionable and threatening behavior ranging from verbal abuse to physical threats. The professor is expected to act as a social worker, dealing with some students who just don't have the ability to pass their courses, let alone the maturity or emotional stability to have to be told this for the first time.

Despite occasional newspaper articles, the issue of grade inflation remained in the background until February 2009, when a report
prepared by Ellen Greenberger at the University of California–Irvine
made national headlines. She found that a third of college students
felt they deserved a B just for showing up in class and 40 percent
said they deserved a B if they completed the required reading for
the class. This report suddenly focused national attention on the
phenomenon of entitled college students who thought they deserved
high grades for doing minimal amounts of work in the classroom.[74]

"I noticed an increasing sense of entitlement in my students
and wanted to discover what was causing it," said Greenberger.
What she found was something that professors had been noticing
for more than a decade. Students thought they should get an A for
effort, even if they didn't score well on tests or write A-level papers.
"Students often confuse the level of effort with the quality of work,"
said James Hogge, associate dean of education at Vanderbilt, in
comments about Greenberger's study. "There is a mentality [among]
students that 'if I work hard, I deserve a high grade.'" When students receive a grade inferior to an A, they often blame the teacher
for being incompetent or unfair.[75]

The Disengagement Compact

In professors' defense, it's impossible to teach students who are
uninterested in learning. I know because I tried to do this for years.
The crisis that pushed higher education into party school land
began in the middle to late 1990s, when increasingly unprepared
and disengaged students began to confront the academic gatekeepers who insisted on high standards. That confrontation created a
culture war that was documented by the National Survey of Student
Engagement, which academia calls Nessie. Over the past decade,
NSSE has asked more than a million American college students at
more than a thousand colleges to fill out an online survey about
their attitudes towards higher education.

In a span of just a few years, NSSE found students' attitudes towards college underwent a significant change. Prior to the culture war, students generally accepted that professors were in charge and set the rules in the classroom and students who didn't conform to those rules would flunk out and not receive a diploma. But during the late 1990s, serious scholars were being replaced by a new cohort who believed they deserved high grades for minimal amounts of work and that working hard was not necessary. In a very short period of time, these new students found themselves in the majority.

Skirmishes broke out in classrooms all over the country as the new students complained that professors were too demanding and made them work too hard. The students also had the ear of the new CEO-wannabe administrators who had been trained to safeguard the college's income sources and concentrate on the retention of students. To get back at professors who set standards that they felt were too high, students savaged teachers on their end-of-class evaluations, which many colleges still use to determine who gets rehired and who gets tenure. Students found that these evaluations were powerful tools and used them to threaten professors who demanded too much of them.

George Kuh, the founder and former director of NSSE, found that at college after college around the country, the culture war was only brought under control by an informal détente or peace treaty, engineered by college administrators to restore order. Kuh has dubbed this "the disengagement compact." Students and professors compromised by adopting an attitude of "I'll leave you alone if you leave me alone." The compact wasn't a formal, written agreement but a kind of cease-fire in the culture war. If professors relax their standards and inflate their grades so that most students can pass, then the students will not complain to administrators or take up valuable office time and will write positive comments on teaching evaluations. In other words, it's exactly what we saw taking place in Brian Strow's class at the beginning of this chapter.

"The existence of this bargain is suggested by the fact that at a relatively low level of effort, many students get decent grades—Bs and sometimes better," Kuh said. "There seems to be a breakdown of shared responsibility for learning—on the part of faculty members who allow students to get by with far less than maximal effort, and on the part of students who are not taking full advantage of the resources institutions provide."[76]

NSSE's surveys found that only 10 percent of American college students were the old-fashioned kind who came to college to learn something. NSSE calls these students "fully engaged." At the other end of the scale they found that 20 percent of students were "fully disengaged." An analysis of NSSE data by two sociology professors, however, found that 40 to 45 percent of students were "fully disengaged." These are the anti-intellectual party school students who chose to spend their time at what *Forbes* magazine dubbed "country club campuses." The remaining 40 to 50 percent of students were in the middle, sometimes engaged and sometimes disengaged. They didn't party all the time but maintained only a minimal interest in their educations.[77] A study conducted by the Higher Education Research Institute at UCLA found similar results: 40 percent of freshmen are disengaged from academic pursuits or alienated from the educational process.[78]

Other experts on higher education use different terms for the same phenomenon. Author and former Indiana University professor Murray Sperber calls it the "nonaggression pact" between faculty and students, where each side agrees not to impinge on the interests of the other. A faculty member who dares to give a student a C, he said, is breaking the pact and can expect a violent reaction from students and complaints from administrators. The teacher will have "to spend a fair amount of time justifying the grade with detailed written comments on the test or exam and a meeting with the upset student." Not surprisingly, most faculty choose not to violate the pact and join the ranks of those who grade more generously.[79]

The resulting decline of academic standards, Sperber said, would be quickly exposed if there were outcome tests for students just before graduation to show how little they have learned in college, but such tests are very rare in academia. "Quality undergraduate education is alive and well in the United States," he said, "it just does not exist for most students at public universities."

The disengagement compact is now nearly universal on party school and subprime college campuses where students are allowed to choose whether they want to learn anything or not. Professors have found from experience or from advice from other professors that fighting the system is a time-consuming and losing battle that can lead to poor job evaluations or denial of tenure. Keeping the students happy at any cost, on the other hand, is encouraged by administrators because it reduces the problems they have to deal with from students and keeps the tuition money rolling in.

How Much Do Students Really Study?

We've seen that students aren't "engaged," but we haven't talked about what this means in terms of actual student work. How much do students really study? The answer: not much.

A number of new reports on successful people have found that the amount of work you do, the amount of time you practice something, the better you become at doing it. Malcolm Gladwell, author of the best-selling book *Outliers*, said ten thousand hours of practice separate the mediocre from the world-class and mentions many successful people, including Mozart, golfer Tiger Woods, and the Beatles, who spent years playing music together eight hours a day in Germany. If you work hard at something, you are likely to get better at it and succeed.[80]

College athletes, musicians, and artists understand this concept and you can see them spending hours in the training room or the studio practicing their skills in order to improve their performances. When it comes to academics, however, college students take a much different attitude. Brought up under the self-esteem movement, they think learning is easy and not worth any effort. It's something you can learn without any hard work. You can simply sit in class and absorb it without reading, writing, or studying.

Colleges were originally set up under the Horatio Alger idea that hours of hard work set students on the road to success. Take students out of the secular society and create an enclave for them where they can pursue their studies without the distractions of the outside world and you can produce the leaders of tomorrow. A generation ago, students were expected to attend classes for fifteen hours a week and study for another thirty hours a week. If they did this for four years, they would rack up some 4,320 hours of academic study, far less than Gladwell's ten thousand hours but well placed on the path to success.

But things are different now. National surveys show that half of American college students spend only nine to fifteen hours a week studying, only half of what was common a generation ago. Because of changes in the curriculum, dumbed-down classes, and lowered expectations, students find they can get by doing very little work and still be rewarded with a grade of B or even A. And instead of being ascetic refuges from the world, today's college campuses are full of distractions like climbing walls, parties, rock concerts, hot tubs, student centers, and high-definition cable television sets that compete with academics for the students' time and attention.

"This is a learned set of behaviors," said Richard Hersh, a former college president, of the few hours students spend studying. "Students are being rewarded for it. They don't do a lot of work but they still get a B. They can buy a paper on the internet and not get caught. No big deal. They can join a fraternity and party five nights a week and then brag about being smashed and still making it through their classes. This is being learned and they get victimized by it."[81]

Instead of teaching them to swim, he said, colleges teach students how to tread water. Students who make a minimal effort manage to stay afloat and not drown but essentially they stay in the same place. "That's a crime," Hersh said.

Kuh said NSSE statistics show that about 20 percent of students are simply drifting through college, yet they don't flunk out and are awarded diplomas. These students have figured out how to game the system to get what they want with the least possible effort. They keep their heads down and avoid attracting attention. They pick large classes and tend to hang together as a group sleepwalking through college.[82] "If this is not higher education's dirty little secret, then it ought to be," said Kuh.

Many of my students in New Hampshire admitted to me that they did no reading or work at all outside of class. They wanted me to set aside time at the end of each class so they could complete their homework assignments. That left them free for the other 95 percent of their time to enjoy the many distractions colleges have to offer. Class time was learning time, but once they left the class, all interest in learning anything was simply turned off.

The University of Maryland, which has been surveying students' study habits for a decade, found that the average amount of time a student spends studying is 14.8 hours per week rather than the 25 hours professors recommend. "It's something that we still preach, but have I ever met a student who does it? Probably not," said Marcy Fallon, director of the University of Maryland's Learning Assistance Service. "As much as we preach it, they're not doing it." She is most concerned about students who take four or five courses a semester but study only six to ten hours a week. "That's a problem," she said.

The Glorification of Stupidity

The college environment rewards minimal studying, but it's not where this sense of entitlement and disinterest in learning comes from. For that, we have to look to our culture.

In 1994, when the members of the college class of 2010 were entering the first grade, a very popular movie was released that won six Oscars, including best picture and best actor. The main character was a lovable idiot who defied all the odds by participating in every major event of his lifetime. His philosophy was that life was just a box of chocolates and you could try out a new self-indulgent treat each day.

A decade and a half later, it seems that Forrest Gump unwittingly spawned an entire generation for whom learning and knowledge are superfluous and who sincerely believe that life will simply hand them their own box of chocolates without any of the hard work that previous generations thought was part of the road to success.

In a 1999 public opinion survey, 55 percent of Americans under the age of thirty said they expected to become rich during their lifetimes. But when interviewers asked a follow-up question about how they expected to acquire that wealth, the answers were vague. Just over 70 percent admitted there was no way they would get rich through their current careers and 76 percent said Americans were not "as willing to work hard at their jobs to get ahead as they were in the past." They also rejected the idea that inheritance or investments would set them on the road to riches.[83]

So how were all of these young Americans going to land on Easy Street? Simple, they said, all it took was a little luck. Good fortune, they said, would inevitably catch up with them and bestow upon them their righteous benefits. Economist Jeremy Rifkin, commenting on the results of this survey, said an entire generation had bought into the mindset that there was no connection between work and success. Younger Americans were "increasingly caught up in the media culture that sold the idea of instant gratification of one's desires" and that "each successive generation of Americans was less willing or even less able to work hard and postpone gratification for future rewards." In fact, he said, today's young narcissists seem to have replaced the classic "American dream" with an "American daydream."[84]

What we are seeing among young people today is the very opposite of the Horatio Alger myth. It's not hard work and climbing up the ladder that leads to success, they say, but becoming a cockeyed optimist and having blind faith that it's just a matter of time before a sudden bolt from the blue will bestow upon them the riches that they rightly deserve. It's the attitude that they might as well have a good time and avoid hard work while killing time waiting until the wheel of fortune smiles upon them. I was baffled by this attitude until I read Barbara Ehrenreich's book *Bright-Sided: How the Relentless Promotion of Positive Thinking Has Undermined America*, in which she describes how millions of Americans have bought into the idea that by simply visualizing what you want—high salaries, yachts, and expensive cars—they will be drawn to you by the near-magical "law of attraction."[85]

So where does education fit into this success-without-work attitude? The old-fashioned mission of education was that it prepared young people with the wisdom, knowledge, and skills they would need to take advantage of opportunities to climb up the ladder to success and to enable them to better understand the world around them. But if today's young people have bought into the belief that they are simply marking time until fortune strikes them, traditional education begins to look like a very boring and very long waste of time. It matches perfectly the attitude that many of today's party school students express. Partying is what you do while waiting for the lightning bolt of success to strike you, and any efforts you make to better yourself are a waste of time and effort. Party school administrators are merely matching their pitch to their customers' needs: *This is the best place to have a good time until the golden arrow of good fortune strikes you.*

None of this is any news to Bart Simpson, the very popular wisecracking cartoon character on *The Simpsons* television program. During the years when today's college students were growing up, Bart was often shown wearing a T-shirt bearing the slogan, "Underachiever and Proud of It!" Bart's slogan has now become the credo of a generation. Learning is for losers, they say. The goal of life is to have a good time and avoid anything that looks like work. Showing interest in a topic in class, asking a question, or even reading the textbook and completing assignments can be social suicide. Students who attempt to follow the "smart track" through school risk being branded forever as nerds who will never be invited to parties or asked out on dates. Some of my smartest students showed me Facebook pages where they were trashed by other students for asking questions in class and reading the textbook.

Although they are exposed to more information than any other generation, thanks to the internet and cable television, survey after survey finds that young people's knowledge and understanding about the world is declining at a rapid rate. Survey after survey during the past five years has shocked observers by revealing just how illiterate recent college graduates are. A December 2005 report called *The National Assessment of Adult Literacy* issued by the federal Department of Education found that only 25 percent of recent college graduates scored high enough to be considered proficient in the use of printed and written information to function in a society.[86]

Doug Hesse, head of the honors program at Illinois State University, said the problem was that the media barraged Americans with flashes and bits of material, sound bites, and factoids, but no one helps them put the facts together and teaches them how to understand them and process them. Colleges tend to do the same thing by asking professors to make their classes more fun, focusing on interesting facts and anecdotes, cut up into easy-to-digest diversions without teaching them to do the hard work: fitting all of this information into real knowledge about the world. Even his honor students, the cream of the crop at American colleges, were assigned an average of fewer than fifty pages of reading per week. "Students seem to spend a lot of time on Facebook, and when you think about the literate practices involved in Facebook, that's probably not contributing a lot to the scores on something like this literacy test."[87]

A generation ago, college upperclassmen were able to read Shakespeare in the original Elizabethan English, understand the writings of Plato and Aristotle, and explain the basics of geology, astronomy, and chemistry. Today, students who study Shakespeare can't understand the plays themselves so they watch movies with Kenneth Branagh as Hamlet, Mickey Rooney as Puck, and Leonardo DiCaprio as Romeo. Few of them have any idea who Plato and Aristotle were or what country or era they were from.

In the years since the literacy survey results were announced in 2005, additional surveys of college seniors tried to narrow down the problem, but the results only got worse. A November 2007 report from the National Endowment for the Arts found that only 22 percent of seventeen-year-olds read anything at all on a given day, down from 31 percent in 1984. It also found that fifteen-to-twenty-four-year-olds spent just seven to ten minutes a day voluntarily reading anything at all.[88]

Many educators have begun warning that the literacy decline of America's college graduates has become a national security issue. How will the United States compete in the world when its college graduates, the leaders of tomorrow, can only read and understand information at an elementary school level? Dana Gioia, chairman of the NEA, in describing the results of the survey, warned that the future economic viability of the United States seemed to be at risk as an illiterate generation took over the reins of power.[89]

Experts agree that the decline has nothing to do with the IQs of young people. Tests show they are just as smart as ever. The problems have to do with attitudes, motivation, and engagement. Many young people today seem to have lost their motivation to learn and are not afraid of going though life without knowing the basics of how their world, their government, or their economy works. The majority of students seem to have none of the curiosity and eagerness to learn that was once the hallmark of incoming college students. They seem to be immune from Aristotle's statement at the beginning of his *Metaphysics* that "all human beings by nature desire to know."

"We are doing a better job of teaching kids to read in elementary school," said one national expert. "But once they enter adolescence, they fall victim to a general culture which does not encourage or reinforce reading. Because these people then read less, they read less well. Because they read less well, they do more poorly in school, in the job market and in civic life . . . This is not a study about literary reading. It's a study about reading of *any* sort and what the consequences of doing it well or doing it badly are. In an increasingly competitive world, the consequences of doing it badly include economic decline. . . . What are the consequences if America becomes a nation in which reading is a minority activity?"[90]

In January 2006, the American Institutes for Research released the results of a survey of 1,827 soon-to-graduate college seniors chosen from eighty colleges around the country. The results, in many ways, were more alarming than the NEA study. It found that most college seniors were unable to understand documents that people encounter every day, such as comparing credit card statements and opposing newspaper editorials. They were unable to compare the cost of food per ounce or interpret the data on a comparison table about exercise and blood pressure. About 20 percent of college seniors had such low levels of quantitative understanding that they could not calculate if a car had enough gas to get to a gas station.[91]

A survey of seniors at the top fifty-five colleges found that only 29 percent knew what "Reconstruction" referred to in American history and only a third could name the American general at the battle of Yorktown. A 1999 survey of teenagers by the National Constitution Center found that only 41 percent could name the three branches of government, even though 59 percent could identify the Three Stooges by name. In a 2003 survey by the Foundation for Individual Rights in Education, only one in fifty students could name the first right guaranteed by the First Amendment and one out of four could not name any freedom protected by it. Other studies found that only 28 percent could name the chief justice of the United States, only 75 percent could name the vice president, only 26 percent could name the secretary of state, and a majority of students could not name the fifty states on an outline map of the country.[92]

Child psychologist Laurence Steinberg, author and critic of public education, has called young people's attitude towards education the "glorification of stupidity." For them, ignorance is nothing to be ashamed of. Students avoid trying too hard because it is a ticket to the land of outcasts and nerds. Without rewards for excellence, anyone who strives to excel begins to look suspect and is shunned by the majority, who are comfortable reveling in the morass of mediocrity. The underachievers are proud of their average status and resist any efforts to push them to try harder.[93]

When anti-intellectual high school graduates with poor reading skills come to college, they bring their "life is only a party" attitudes with them. The difference, of course, is that at college the playground set up by Diplomas Inc. is much larger and more expensive and there are no parents to set any limits. Although there are still dedicated and engaged students who attend college—even party schools—the students who fail to measure up academically often devalue education and believe that what they are learning is essentially worthless. Students in my classes repeatedly expressed this anti-intellectual attitude. They told me that they already knew everything they needed to know and were not interested in learning what I was supposed to teach them. They felt there was absolutely no connection between learning and success, no matter how much I tried to explain it to them.

"Most students feel compelled to stay in school, but there is also a widespread sense that much of what goes on there is irrelevant to their futures," wrote sociologists Côté and Allahar. "Young people now have many more interesting and pleasurable distractions, against which book learning does not stand a chance except among a few outstanding students dismissed by the student culture as nerds or brains. . . . Some students increasingly act like self-entitled consumers demanding satisfaction," they said.[94]

"These anti-intellectual behaviors and attitudes are now so rife on college campuses that motivated and engaged students are being squelched by them," said Paul Trout, an English professor at Montana State University. Obsessed with their hair, their clothes, their cars, their boyfriends and girlfriends, and how many friends they have on Facebook, they have little that could be recognized as an intellectual life.[95]

While there have always been students who were bored with college, Trout said, "What has changed is the *number* of students who exhibit these attitudes." Although no one has actually counted them, the number seems to be growing and they have reached a critical mass where they refuse to read the material for class and many of them even fail to show up. "If colleges and universities wind up providing comfortable environments for more and more slackers and screw-offs," Trout said, colleges "will likely surrender whatever is left of their academic integrity and social credibility. Faced with growing numbers of high school graduates who resent and resist the rigors, demands, and pleasures of higher education, colleges and universities have lowered standards to keep students happy and enrollments up."[96]

The Tragedy of the 10 Percent

During my twelve years as a college instructor, there was only one small group of students who ever complained about the decline in academic standards: the smart, fully engaged students who expected to be intellectually stimulated in college and were extremely disappointed at what they were getting for their money. There were consistently two to four of these students in each of my classes and nearly all of them were miserable. The skimpy reading assignments, the low level of classroom discussion, the time wasted taking attendance, and going over the same material time and again all irritated them.

Instead of making comments or asking questions in class, which was frowned on by other students, they would often show up in my office after class to talk about what should have been discussed in class. In the strange world of Diplomas Inc., intellectual discussions must be conducted in secret, out of the way of the general party school climate.

It's these students, the ones who went to college because they were intellectual, curious, and interested in learning about the world, who are being most cheated. Many of them transfer to more demanding colleges during freshman year. They chose the party school or subprime college, they said, because it was close to home or because the tuition was lower, but it was not providing them with what they needed and wanted. They were appalled by the lack of intellectual stimulation and any kind of rigor or challenge. They hated the easy grading policies that made them feel like chumps for working hard. They complained about the lack of any clearly defined goals. They complained that the A that they received was made worthless by the high grades that the slackers received. "Why should I work hard if someone else does nearly nothing and gets the same grade?" they asked.

The two or three students in each class who were enthusiastic about journalism and wanted to be crusading reporters who exposed evil-doers and celebrated unknown heroes felt cheated. These students didn't need a course in third-grade grammar. They were talented writers who worked on their high school newspapers and wanted to take their writing skills to the next level. They wanted to learn how to conduct interviews, how to improve their writing and reporting, and how to write the best leads. They were the kinds of students I expected to teach when I first accepted the job.

This always created a dilemma for me, as it did for hundreds of other professors I have spoken with around the country. Did you teach the class at a high level for the few enthusiastic and engaged students who really wanted to learn or did you dumb it down for the majority who were not the least bit interested in listening to what you had to say? If you dumbed down the class and invented games and told jokes to entertain the disengaged students, the engaged students rightfully complained that the class was aimed too low. If you aimed higher, the disengaged students simply tuned you out.

When I was appointed advisor for some of these students with high expectations, my advice was that they transfer to a better college where they would not have to deal with such anti-intellectual harassment.

During my last year at the college, a new honors program was established to deal with this dilemma. The upper 10 percent of the students would be culled from the rest of the population and enrolled in special programs with special classes. The idea was that these students, many of whom probably chose to attend a party school by mistake and could have gone somewhere more demanding, could be taught at a higher level, something approximating the college level of a generation ago.

The unintended consequence, as was pointed out during discussions of this plan, was that the remaining vast majority of students enrolled at the college would be taught at the elementary school level. They'd learn how to read a single 150-page book in English class. They'd learn to do long division in math and how to find the United States on a world map in geography class. It would be all remediation all the time.

For most of the professors I spoke with, the upper 10 percent students were the only satisfying part of their jobs. They felt like someone was actually listening and learning. These students were the ones who went out and got good jobs in their fields and came back to thank us for teaching them. They were a source of pride.

The vast majority of my students, however, were employed after graduation as clerks and waiters. Whenever I encountered them in these jobs where they were making absolutely no use of the skills I taught them, I would ask them what had happened. Most of them were vague and unwilling to discuss how they were paying off their student loans. The ones who did open up said they were still waiting for their big break, for the fickle finger of success to bestow its wealth upon them.

4

Party School Perils

Just before the students returned for the fall 2008 semester at Keene State College in New Hampshire, the city newspaper ran an article about preparations to welcome them back. The article wasn't about back-to-school sales or new programs or student fashions. Instead, the headline was this:

Police prepare for college
Arrests are expected to rise[97]

The city was set to welcome the students the way a medieval village prepared for a raid by the Vikings. Head for the hills! Lock up your daughters! The students are coming! The police chief outlined for the newspaper his strategic plan to marshal his forces and prepare to meet the onslaught. Police officers were being put on overtime. Some were preparing to go undercover in student garb to act as the point men. Officers were assigned bicycles so they could catch students who ran away when approached.

No one even suggested that any of this was an overreaction. The chief cited figures that arrests for crimes like public intoxication, assault, rape, noise, and public urination went up significantly when the students arrived. It wasn't just the thousands of additional residents, he said, but a different *kind* of resident, much more likely to disturb the peace. During the 2006–2007 school year, he noted, there were 1,430 arrests in the quiet New England city, 359 of which, or about 25 percent, involved someone connected with the college.

Just four days after the article was published, the chief's predictions about drunken mayhem proved correct. Philip Bantz, a reporter for the *Keene Sentinel*, spent the night with undercover police officers as they patrolled the midnight party scene just outside the campus walls.

Long after the adult citizens had turned in for the night, a strange kind of vampire culture appeared on the streets. The officers told Bantz it was common to find groups of young men standing together and urinating on a lawn while young women in skimpy outfits "beat the heck out of each other in the middle of the street." The problems begin when drunken students pour out of house parties with beer and hard liquor in their ubiquitous red plastic cups. "All of a sudden it just totally explodes," a policeman told Bantz. "It's like an algae bloom." When the officers confront students, the most common thing for them to do is to run away, especially the majority of them who are younger than twenty-one.

When the officers caught a twenty-year-old student with a cup of beer, he told police that his parents would pull him out of school when they heard about his arrest. The officers were not sympathetic and the student was charged with unlawful possession of alcohol, put in handcuffs, and taken to the police station. Police used to issue appearance tickets in these kinds of situations, but now they go through a formal arrest. "If we let them go with a slap on the wrist, they'd turn around and do it again," the policeman said. "People don't want to see you peeing. No one wants to wake up and find beer cans all over their lawn. And when you have that many drunk people together you're going to have fights, thefts, sexual assaults, you name it."

Police arrested fifteen students that night for crimes that included public intoxication, resisting arrest, and open container violations. A local high school boy, age sixteen, was arrested after he had passed out from drinking on the back porch of a college student's house. His parents were called at 4:30 A.M. and were asked to pick him up at the police station. Another student kicked out the window of a city business, lacerating a tendon in his ankle. Police found him unconscious at 2:40 A.M. lying on the ground with a shirt wrapped around his bleeding ankle. Police told Bantz that, despite those arrests, it was considered a slow night.[98]

During other weekends, local public safety officials told me they had had to deal with a student who had passed out from drinking on a winter night and was found frozen to the asphalt of a parking lot. On some weekends, the student parties at local houses spill out into the street, where cars and couches are set on fire and students throw rocks and bottles at police. In the fall of 2009, an eighteen-year-old student called police on her cell phone to say she was hanging from the rafters of an abandoned building after falling through the roof. After she was rescued, she told police she had gone up on the roof to watch the sunrise—at 8:20 A.M. She was arrested after police found a marijuana pipe in her pocket.

During my dozen years as a college newspaper adviser, my students wrote about attempted suicides, drug overdoses, students firing BB guns at students from their dormitory windows, students knifed at fraternity parties, and students raped in their dormitory rooms. On Sunday morning, the campus was usually littered with trash and abandoned red cups, beer cans, and liquor bottles.

Although most parents aren't aware of it, college campuses and the communities around them are among the most dangerous places in America, rivaling inner cities in the number of crimes committed per acre. There is no mystery about why this happens. Take thousands or even tens of thousands of adolescents with limitless free time, fill them to the brim with alcohol and other drugs, take away all parental and teacher supervision, and what you get is an instant crime wave. Assaults, arsons, rapes, vandalism, hate crimes, sexual harassment, auto break-ins, burglaries, and thefts take place every week in the area around party school campuses. College administrators and local police are well aware of this problem, but parents, misled by the reassuring but totally incorrect number of crimes listed on the college's official website, have no idea of the risks to which their children are being exposed.

When they are in high school, students are constantly and carefully supervised by parents and teachers. Students who misbehave are grounded, sent to detention, or called into a meeting with their parents to discuss their patterns of behavior. But once they are safely behind the college gates, students enter a supervision vacuum. The policy at most colleges is that students are eighteen and therefore legally adults, capable of making their own decisions. But at party schools, the vast majority of students are adults in name only. Psychologically and developmentally, most of these students are still immature adolescents desperately in need of someone in authority to set limits on their behavior. With no one watching over them, most college students simply run wild and repeatedly damage themselves and each other. Students with medical problems suddenly stop taking their medications. They stay up all night and sleep all day, missing their classes. When they are bored, they pull the fire alarm to drum up some excitement. They brutally attack each other physically and sexually and have to be rushed to the hospital following overdoses of alcohol and drugs. None of this is the kind of behavior you would expect from mature adults. College campuses are among the few places in America where this kind of behavior is openly tolerated.

Most college students remain dangerously immature and unable to make the most basic choices about whether to attend classes, do their homework, study for tests, use drugs, engage in unsafe sex, or drink themselves into unconsciousness. Parents are seriously uninformed about this. They mistakenly think that party school administrators will call them as soon as there is any sign of a problem, just as high school administrators did. Parents are deliberately kept in the dark about their children's misbehavior until the problem becomes a catastrophe. The hands-off policy on student behavior allows party school administrators to avoid any blame when things go wrong. Most colleges and universities have a policy of not even informing parents if students are arrested, attacked, attempt suicide, or receive treatment for alcohol or drug abuse.

Administrators claim this policy is to protect the students' privacy, but the real reason is that allowing students to have the time of their lives at college is part of the prime mission of party schools: retention, retention, retention of happy, tuition-paying customers. Set too many restrictive rules and the customers will take their business elsewhere. Administrators know that students consider calling parents a form of "snitchin'," which they find very uncool.

Where Binge Drinkers Rule

The centerpiece of party school life is drinking. It's difficult to overestimate how important drinking is in the life of a party school student. It's not just what they do when they are sitting down with friends at a party or watching television or playing music or video games. It is an activity unto itself, an essential part of everyday life and the dating ritual, the basic lubricant that fuels interactions with other people, and an escape route from boredom, stress, conflict, or emotional distress. Beer and hard liquor are available everywhere twenty-four hours a day on campus and off campus, even though it is illegal even to possess it for the 85 percent of college students who are under the age of twenty-one.

"With so few hours filled with learning, boredom sets in and students have to find something to pass the time. Instead of learning, they drink," said Stuart Rojstaczer, a former Duke professor and author of books on grade inflation.[99]

The five-year party starts even before the first members of the freshman class set foot on campus at the end of the summer. During their senior year at high school, local students attend the nightly parties in the student ghettos and fraternity houses around the campuses. The high school students usually have to go home long before the party ends because their parents are waiting up for them, but they begin to count the days until they too can fully participate in the college party scene.

In 2008, my students showed me Facebook pages with the name of my college and "Class of 2009" next to it. This was where high school seniors planned their futures as party school binge drinkers. A main point of discussion on the page was whether dress-up parties were appropriate during any weekend or only at Halloween. They were already planning their first parties for the night of move-in day, over a year ahead of time. Nowhere on these pages was there any mention of academics or classes or majors or professors. It was all about the party.

Freshman orientation programs have also become initiations into the party school lifestyle. At the University of New Hampshire, a student-run camp set up to welcome new students to campus was put on probation in 2004 after upperclassmen gave beer to the underage incoming freshmen. The camp continued to operate until 2008, when the college shut it down permanently after reports of lewd skits, including public nudity. One student deliberately urinated on herself and other female students lifted up their shirts to display their breasts for first-year students.[100]

This kind of freshmen orientation only makes sense once you understand that it's all part of the way party schools market themselves to high school students. Although they can't advertise it directly, they get the message out to high school students that college is where you go to drink yourself into oblivion for five years. Classes don't matter. No one expects you to learn anything. Friends will help you get by with a minimum amount of work and help you choose the classes and professors who won't require any work. You can borrow as much money as you need to pay your bills. The important thing is to have a good time and don't let anything get in the way of the five-year party.

Drinking has become a part of the mating ritual for college students looking to "hook up" or "shack" with another student. Students, both male and female, said drinking "loosened them up" and made them more social and less intimidated during the sometimes awkward process of sorting out who is going home with whom after a night at a bar or a party. Because buying enough drinks at a bar to become intoxicated can be expensive, many students said they indulged in "pre-party," which involves drinking at home to the point of intoxication and then going out to the local bar to meet people. This easing of the barriers, however, comes dangerously close to the definition of date rape.[101] When I talk with parents of college students about binge drinking, their immediate reaction is to dismiss it. They think that the news media is exaggerating the problem. "What's so bad if the kids want to have a beer while they're watching football on TV or have a drink with their friends? What's wrong with having a drink? Why don't they just lighten up and let the kids have a good time?" is a typical response.

But binge drinking has nothing to do with sipping a beer in a dorm room. Binge drinking is when a student kneels down on the floor and places a rubber hose in his mouth; the hose is attached at the other end to a funnel, which is filled by another student from a beer keg or a vodka bottle. This apparatus allows the alcohol to bypass the swallowing reflex and pass directly into the stomach to be absorbed by the bloodstream. It's not just an attempt to get as drunk as possible in the shortest amount of time; it's a dangerous form of physical abuse that allows students to pass through the intoxicated stage directly into unconsciousness.

"That is idiocy," said Dee Owens, president of the Indiana Coalition to Reduce Underage Drinking, of the students who drink to pass out. "That is not drinking. That is not socially interacting and having fun." She said she has increasingly seen students who had blood alcohol levels of two or even three times the legal limit, which can cause brain damage and even death.[102]

The binge drinking that takes place at party schools is as different from social drinking as a shoving match is from a nuclear attack. Binge drinking is defined as five or more drinks in a row for men and four or more drinks in a row for women. In a survey of students at 119 American colleges, Harvard University found that 44 percent of American college students had engaged in binge drinking during the two weeks before the survey. The figures were higher for men (51 percent) than women (40 percent). These statistics were for all kinds of colleges around the country, including many non-party colleges where education is taken seriously. At the kind of party schools described in this book, binge drinkers are a solid majority. The typical binge drinker was white, middle class, age twenty-three or younger, and a member of a fraternity or sorority. If they were binge drinkers in high school, according to the survey, they were three times more likely to be binge drinkers in college.[103] But beyond regular binge drinkers, there is a more serious group called the super binge drinkers, who became intoxicated three or more times in a two-week period. Over half of the binge drinkers, or about 23 percent of all college students, fell into this category.

The collegiate culture of drinking seems to be moving from keg parties to industrial-strength guzzling, with a full third of our nation's colleges and universities qualifying as high binge drinking campuses where more than half the students indicated in surveys that they were binge drinkers. The rate was much higher among Greeks, where 86 percent of fraternity brothers and 80 percent of sorority sisters were classified as binge drinkers.[104]

One college ritual that is particularly deadly is the tradition of students drinking twenty-one shots of liquor on their twenty-first birthdays. This feat is basically impossible for most people to achieve without alcohol poisoning, but it doesn't keep students from trying, often with deadly results. In October 2007, for example, Amanda Jax, a student at Minnesota State, died of alcohol poisoning on her twenty-first birthday while attempting to down twenty-one drinks at a bar.[105]

Drinking is, in fact, often an end in itself, as shown by the number of party games or beer games that students described for me. Among the most popular drinking games at my college was "Beirut," which was also referred to as "beer pong" on other campuses. It consists of setting up red plastic sixteen-ounce plastic cups on both ends of a table and throwing ping-pong balls so that they land inside the cups on the other side. When a ball lands in a cup, the defending team must drink the beer in that cup.[106]

While some colleges have attempted to ban the game, most party school administrators simply look the other way. They know that it is being played but do little to stop it, even when it is played on campus, often as part of leagues and championships, the results of which are posted on dormitory walls. At my college, special ping-pong balls with the college logo were sold in the campus store right next to the college-imprinted shot glasses and beer mugs. When I asked one of the clerks why the ping-pong balls were displayed next to the shot glasses, she explained to me that the balls were used for a drinking game and were never meant to be used on a ping-pong table. So although the college's official policy is to discourage binge drinking, administrators can't resist the temptation to profit from it when they get a chance.

In the summer of 2005, the Anheuser-Busch Companies, the brewers of Budweiser and Bud Light, two of the most popular beers among college students, began marketing "Bud Pong" kits through beer distributors. The company, which has an official policy of discouraging binge drinking and drinking by minors, set up promotions in college bars using special beer pong cups and table covers.[107]

When the *New York Times* caught wind of this, it contacted Francine Katz, vice president for communications and consumer affairs for Anheuser-Busch, and asked why the company was violating its policies by encouraging underage drinking and binge drinking. Katz said she wasn't aware that students were using the game to drink beer. The game, she said, was designed to be used with water and not beer!

The *Times* then followed up by asking college-town bar owners across the country what liquid had been used to fill the cups. A bartender near Clemson University said she had worked at a number of Bud Pong events and never saw a game where the cups were filled with water. Henry Wechsler, director of the College Alcohol Study at the Harvard School of Public Health, questioned why a company that sold alcohol would promote games that involve drinking water. "It's preposterous," he told the *Times*.

Just three days after the *Times* story appeared, Anheuser-Busch announced that it was withdrawing its support for Bud Pong. "Despite our explicit guidelines," Katz said, "there may have been instances where this promotion was not carried out in the manner it was intended."[108]

Despite their official policies of discouraging binge drinking, the sales departments of brewing and distilling companies have been working closely with college administrators to target college students as the next generation of customers. Sports stadiums and auditoriums used for rock concert halls, for example, are full of advertising for alcohol with money flowing from the brewers directly into college treasuries. A reporter for the student newspaper at Berkeley charged that she and her fellow students were being deliberately targeted through their colleges by big alcohol.[109]

Another popular pastime is making Jell-O shots, in which vodka or some other form of hard alcohol is substituted for the water in making regular Jell-O. The finished product tastes like flavored gelatin with barely a trace of alcohol taste. This makes it popular with inexperienced drinkers who down several of them in a few minutes and quickly become intoxicated. Dozens of websites are dedicated to recipes for making them.

A student can drink two cans of beer in only two seconds using the drinking funnel or a similar apparatus made out of a plastic gasoline can. The liquid is ingested continuously rather than sipping as one would do if drinking normally. When there is no funnel around, students can achieve some of the same speed of consumption by a process called "shotgunning." This involves punching a hole in the side of a beer can with a knife. The drinker then places his lips to the hole, tilts the can right side up and pops the top. This causes the beer to be forced through the hole quickly. The entire contents of the can empty into the student's mouth in five seconds or less.

Unconscious students are so common on party school campuses that students have a name for them: furniture. Some thoughtful students use what's called the "Bacchus maneuver" (after the Greek god of wine) to turn unconscious students onto their sides to prevent them from suffocating on their own vomit. Some less thoughtful students use permanent markers to write messages on the unconscious student's skin.

In many college towns, requests to take unconscious students to the hospital make up over half of the city's total number of ambulance calls. At Penn State, for example, the nation's number one party school, the number of students taken to the hospital for alcohol poisoning increased 84 percent in three years to 585.[110] At the college I taught at in New Hampshire, there were so many false fire alarms and ambulance calls for drunken students that the city required the college to pay a fee to support the expensive public services consumed by all those drunken students.

Managing Binge Drinkers

Because most student drinking parties take place off campus and in fraternity houses, they are mostly out of the direct control of the college. The drinking that takes place on campus, although significant, is much more hidden. Students told me it was never a problem to obtain beer and liquor in any dorm on campus at any time of day or night. Most of the students I spoke with had phony ID cards that showed they were over twenty-one when they were really only nineteen. There were students with machines that could alter the birth date on your driver's license, but most students simply acquired someone else's license. The clerks at the store only looked at the date, not the picture. The bouncers in the local bars had drawers full of fake IDs that did not quite pass the test.

It's difficult to control the flow of alcohol on a campus because many of the seniors are over the age limit. Seniors can buy as much beer and hard liquor as they want legally and then bring it back to the dorms or houses in the off-campus student ghetto to resell at a handsome profit. But the biggest obstacle to controlling binge drinking is that party school administrators understand that binge drinkers make up a majority of their customers and sending them packing or making them unhappy would be a very poor business decision. Binge drinkers and party schools exist in one of those symbiotic relationships that party schools find so convenient. As long as they pay their tuition, binge drinkers looking for the five-year party are welcome, but administrators have to play a careful balancing act when the antics of drunken students hit the front pages. Taking any kind of serious action against binge drinkers could change their reputation at student-run websites from *party school* to *unfriendly to drinking* and leave them with nearly empty classrooms and dormitory halls. The majority of students simply don't want to go to a college that won't let them drink themselves into unconsciousness, so a reputation for being unfriendly to drinking is a suicidal marketing position.

Most students see excessive drinking as a major part of the college experience. For those reasons, administrators pretend to get tough on bingers but are careful not to get tough enough to scare students away. They usually sit on their hands until parents, local residents, or the local newspaper demand that they do something.

They issue press releases telling the public that they are serious about disciplining their inebriated scholars, but the students understand that this is all just smoke and mirrors and that the college isn't really going to cancel the party.

A typical penalty for students who are arrested for alcohol violations is to send them to a college-run alcohol education program, which no one really thinks does any good, especially the students. It's like sending Paris Hilton to rehab. My student journalists wrote articles about students who took the hour-long course and then went out and celebrated by "getting really fucked up" at a post-class bash held in their honor.

The administrators who run party schools regularly attend workshops to discuss student binge drinking and what they can do about it. What would seem to be the simplest solution—expelling binge drinkers—is not an option because it would interfere with their prime directive: retention of students. Tough punishments are out for the same reason. Instead, what college administrators seem to learn about at these conferences is how to keep the public from finding out what is going on. This works most of the time—until there is a tragedy that is too big to sweep under the rug.

In 1997, for example, Scott Krueger, a freshman at MIT, died of alcohol poisoning. During his autopsy, it was found that the amount of alcohol in his blood was five times the legal limit in Massachusetts. Since then, thousands of college students have been found dead of alcohol overdoses. Colleges inform the parents, schedule a candlelight memorial vigil, set up counseling sessions, and then try to move the story off the front pages before it can cause any more damage to college applications.

The National Institute on Alcohol Abuse and Alcoholism estimated that 1,700 college students die every year as a result of alcohol abuse, including alcohol poisoning, automobile accidents, and assaults. Another six hundred thousand are injured as a result of drinking. Nearly seven hundred thousand students are assaulted by other students and four hundred thousand reported having unsafe sex while intoxicated. There are one hundred thousand sexual assaults or date rapes each year while one of the parties is intoxicated and another hundred thousand students reported that they had sexual activity but were too intoxicated to remember if they had given consent or not.[111] The Institute found that 25 percent of college students reported academic consequences from drinking, including missing classes, falling behind, doing poorly on exams, and receiving lower grades.[112]

The physical damage, however, may not show up until years after graduation. A recent study by the Bowles Center for Alcohol Studies at the University of North Carolina found that binge drinking by young people can cause brain damage that persists far into the adult years, long after the binge drinking has stopped. After they stopped drinking and became sober, adult rats in this study could still learn, but they could not relearn information. Normal rats that had learned to find food in a particular place could easily go to a new spot when the food was moved. But rats that had been given excessive amounts of alcohol in their youth kept returning to the place where the food had been and were unable to find food in a different location. This damage affected adolescents more than adults and resulted in diminished control over cravings for alcohol and poor decision-making. Normal adolescent brains were programmed for accelerated learning and how to make decisions when faced with ambiguity, but when large doses of alcohol were added, this accelerated learning did not take place.[113]

Even Nondrinkers Are Victims

Even the 20 percent of college students who do not drink at all, either for religious, moral, or health reasons, felt the impact of the problem. At colleges with high binge drinking rates (that is, the party schools), 71 percent of students said they had their sleep interrupted by drunken students; 57 percent said they had to take care of an intoxicated student; 36 percent said they had been insulted or humiliated by a drunken student; 23 percent had experienced an unwanted sexual encounter with a drunken student; 23 percent had had a serious argument with a drunken student; 16 percent had had personal property damaged by a drunken student; 11 percent had been pushed, hit, or assaulted; and 1 percent had been the victim of sexual advance, assault, or date rape.[114]

This silent minority of nondrinking students has become increasingly disgusted with the immature behavior of the boisterous majority and the peer pressure it puts on nonbingers. Meredith Austin Granwehr, then a junior at University of Connecticut, one of New England's most notorious party schools, wrote about her frustrations in an op-ed piece published in the *Hartford Courant*. Walking through the college social scene without the ubiquitous red plastic cup, she said, makes her the target of other students encouraging her to drink up.[115]

"My generation seems to have the frightening conception that extreme binge drinking, to the point of blacking out, is the key ingredient for a good time," she wrote. "Sadly, this trend is spiraling out of control, carrying grave consequences with it."

During her first weekend back at school in September 2007, she said, she saw three students being taken to the emergency room on stretchers because of their excessive drinking. Among the newest fads, she said, was mixing alcohol with caffeine-based energy drinks like Red Bull to mask the effects of intoxication and make students think they are more sober than they really are. This leads students to drink even more excessively and to think they can drive a car while impaired.

"My generation loves to overindulge," she wrote. "Unfortunately, our obsession with excessive consumption of alcohol carries severe consequences. Even if one does not die from binge drinking, it is sad to think that someone may not remember the events of the previous might, or worse, remember something she wishes she could forget."

Parents, she said, have no idea what their children are doing at college. They think that a little underage drinking is just "being a typical college kid," but are clueless about the amounts and the ways students are drinking and how dangerous it is. She thought parents and administrators needed to be more involved in efforts to curb the binge drinking epidemic on campus. Without that assistance, she said, her peers were likely to become members of a "wasted generation."

Nondrinking students like Meredith are under enormous pressure from their drinking peers to neglect their studies and join the party. The mother of a college student wrote to Dear Abby in 2008, relating how her freshman daughter, Christie, was having trouble studying when her roommate and suitemates were drinking constantly and not going to classes: "This makes my daughter not only unhappy but isolated." Abby suggested that her daughter try transferring to a different dormitory with more serious students and try to find a study group for serious students.[116]

Parents of students headed for college are becoming more alarmed by the amount of abusive drinking that takes place, according to a 2008 poll. More than half of parents said they are less likely to send their children to a known party school and 70 percent said they wanted colleges to inform them if their child violates alcohol policies. However, as we will see in the next chapter, most colleges refuse to notify parents of any kind of disciplinary violation, citing confidentiality rules. Three-quarters of parents said they supported stricter enforcement of existing alcohol rules, but only a tiny minority of students felt the same way.[117]

Henry Wechsler, the nation's recognized expert on college student alcohol abuse, advised parents to "put pressure on schools" to explain what they are doing to solve the problem. On campus tours, he said, parents should ask to examine dormitories to look for signs of alcohol abuse such as excessive noise and vomit in bathrooms.[118]

Racism, Sexism, and Homophobia

The Center for Science in the Public Interest, which spoke with college presidents around the country about binge drinking, concluded that it is the most serious problem on college campuses today, not just on its own, but because it contributes to many other problems. According to C. D. Mote, president of the University of Maryland, "Virtually every sexual assault is associated with alcohol abuse. Almost every assault of any kind is related to drinking."[119] But drinking alone isn't responsible for such behavior. A culture of prejudice and disrespect, allowed by a lack of discipline by administrators, does the rest.

Barrett Seaman, the author of *Binge: What Your College Student Won't Tell You*, spent a year talking with students at elite colleges around the country and was surprised to find very few racist, sexist, and homophobic remarks. "What I found instead was a vast majority of students well schooled in the need to show ethnic and gender sensitivity and who seemed anxious to avoid any kind of confrontation," he said.[120]

At party schools, however, racism, sexism, and homophobia are alive and well. Mark Potok, director of the Southern Poverty Law Center, which monitors hate crimes, said college campuses are the third leading location for hate crimes, after homes and highways.[121]

Young people are viewed as more racially tolerant because schools have taught them about multi-culturalism and diversity since they were children, said Melissa Harris-Lacewell, an African American studies expert from Princeton. "On the other hand, young people lack impulse control, drink heavily and stand around outside."[122]

In October 2005, Steve Wessler, the executive director of the Center for the Prevention of Hate Violence, conducted a series of focus groups at Keene State College in New Hampshire, a college that has a black president but whose student body is 98 percent white. Students had scrawled the word *nigger* across the front of a poster advertising Black History Month events and there had been complaints about harassment of Muslin students, gay students, handicapped students, and women. Incidents of racial, ethnic, and gender harassment including graffiti, verbal slurs, and threats were reported. A female teacher reported that she had been sexually harassed by a male student. The college hired Wessler to find out what was going on.[123]

Wessler's report was a wake-up call for the campus. Bias and prejudice are deep-seated, he said. On a daily basis both male and female students hear male students use sexually degrading words about women. A number of Jewish students said they were uncomfortable being openly Jewish on campus.

Women were commonly referred to as *hos*, *bitches*, and *cunts* in regular conversations. Many female professors told Wessler that they were often afraid of attacks in their classrooms from male students who treated them with a lack of respect and courtesy. In their anonymous evaluations of faculty at the end of the semester, students used sexually suggestive terms about teachers' bodies.

Black students were called *niggers*. Muslim students were called *terrorists* and gay students were called *dykes*, *queers*, and *fags*. The responses revealed widespread and casual use of racist, sexist, anti-Semitic, and homophobic jokes and language, hierarchical attitudes of faculty towards staff and students towards faculty, and unwanted touching of women's breasts and buttocks, leading to feelings of isolation, self-hatred, and fear for the targets.

The report told of students calling a convenience store clerk the *Iraqi Paki* and Jews *cheap*. It listed racial slurs and described a student who writes poems about his hatred of black people, which usually end with them dying. He reads these poems aloud at parties. One woman recalled several men following her around campus and yelling "Go back to India, bitch!" One of my students wrote a news article in which he ridiculed students who were blind or who used wheelchairs on campus. A female student told Wessler she was sexually assaulted and nearly raped twice in the same night. After listing page after page of this kind of behavior, Wessler concluded his report by saying that Keene State was not all that different from other colleges he had studied. In other words, the things he found were common on most college campuses.

Although party schools pay a lot of lip service to politically correct topics like multi-culturalism and diversity, they rarely make policy decisions that would enforce those ideas. At my college, a requirement that all liberal arts students learn a foreign language was scrapped because students said they thought it was too much work. Party schools' commitments to diversity turned out to be not as important as the bottom line. Over and over again, party schools advocate for a politically correct concept like diversity but then refuse to take action against students who participate in the campus culture of racism, sexism, and homophobia. They allow students to get away with illegal and immoral misbehavior in the name of retention. Perhaps nowhere is this more evident than in the way party schools deal with rape.

Date Rape

Police declined to take any action in response to a gang rape complaint filed in 2006 by Megan Wright, a student at Dominican College in New York, against three of her fellow students. Rapes take place all the time on college campuses, but what makes Wright's case exceptional is that there was a video camera in the hallway outside the dorm room where the alleged crime took place. The camera showed Megan and the three men, all of them obviously intoxicated, returning from an off-campus party and entering the room.

A few moments later, one of the three men stood in front of the camera with a sign, supposedly signed by Wright, reading "I want to have sex." After the incident, Wright went to the hospital, where an examination found physical evidence that she had been raped. But the school refused to prosecute the case because it said it did not have enough evidence against the three men named in her complaint. The sign, the police said, was evidence that Wright had given consent to have sex, even though Wright said she did not write on the sign.

Denied a trial, Wright was forced to attend classes and eat in the dining hall with the men she said had raped her. Her mother said Wright became increasingly depressed, which led her to take her own life seven months after the incident. Wright's mother hired celebrity lawyer Gloria Allred and filed a lawsuit against the college for failure to prosecute the case, which has become a cause célèbre among college rape activists and was even featured on a segment of the *Dr. Phil* show called "Campus Crisis."[124]

Because of the nature of the crime, it's incredibly difficult to calculate the number of date rapes that occur on college campuses each year. Date rape is a crime in which the victim may not even be aware that she has been attacked and victims are often reluctant to talk about what happened, even anonymously. A *New York Times* report estimated that the number of women raped or sexually assaulted at colleges ranged from one in seven to one in twenty-five.[125] Another study found that one in twelve college men admitted to forcing a woman to have sexual intercourse against her will.[126]

In December 2009, the Center for Public Integrity, an investigative journalism group based in Washington, DC, produced a lengthy report called "Sexual Assault on Campus" that found that one in five campus women are victims of rape or attempted rape by the time they graduate. The report said colleges try to discourage victims from filing complaints and deliberately falsify their crime reports to make campuses appear much safer than they really are.[127]

The "stop snitchin'" gangsta culture that dominates campus life frowns on students who file crime complaints with police. Serial date rapists can therefore usually count on their victims being "cool" and suffering in silence. Typically, a college rape victim is conflicted about making a report because she feels unsure whether she "sent the wrong message" or was not clear about her intentions before the rape. Women often feel that they might have led the man on, especially if both of them were intoxicated. A typical date rape, students told me, came about when two students, one male and the other female, were walking home from a party or a bar. The man assumes that this is an agreement to have sex although the woman does not or perhaps changes her mind as she becomes more sober. There is then a confrontation and unwanted sex occurs.

Even those victims like Megan Wright who were brave enough to file complaints find that colleges set numerous roadblocks in the way of justice. Many victims complain that campus security offices actually discourage them from filing complaints by telling them that if they had been drinking that night they are "unreliable witnesses." It would be their word against that of their attackers. This is, of course, total nonsense. According to the definition of rape in most states, an intoxicated person cannot give consent to sex. So any victim who has sex while drunk is, by definition, a rape victim. By that line of thinking, about 90 percent of women have been raped at least once in college.

Colleges are required by federal law to list on their websites the number of rapes that are reported, but as we will see in the next chapter, party schools deliberately falsify these reports for public relations purposes. My student journalists told me that date rape is a very common occurrence that rarely gets reported. After all, if you concentrate five thousand to twenty thousand adolescents in an area of a few acres and figure that about 40 percent of them are intoxicated at any one time, date rape is perhaps the inevitable result. When I asked my student reporters about why so few rapes are reported, many of them mentioned the Kobe Bryant incident, in which the alleged victim's name and photo were posted on the internet and she became a target of ridicule and hatred. No college student, even one who has been attacked and injured, wants to risk that kind of public scorn. Victims also said that if they reported a rape by a fraternity brother or a star athlete, the authorities were more likely to believe the powerful male than the unknown female.

College women told author Alan DeSantis that most rapes were never reported. "It's like ridiculous the number of rapes that happen on campus," a sorority vice president named Nancy told him. Janis, another of DeSantis's informants, said she knew a woman who was raped by a "big man on campus" and never reported it because it would just be her word against his.[128]

Women students told me that date rape drugs, widely available from campus drug dealers, were a major concern. Although there are several drugs, including animal tranquilizers, the most popular are Rohypnol pills, popularly known as "roofies." The verb "to roofie" refers to someone dropping this drug into a woman's drink, where it quickly dissolves in the alcohol. Someone who consumes a drink that has a roofie in it becomes incapacitated, and bystanders may simply assume that the person is drunk. The drug takes effect about fifteen minutes after it is consumed and can cause amnesia, so victims are often unable to remember what happened to them. Roofie victims find it almost impossible to report the crime to police when they have nothing other than suspicions on which to base their complaints.

Party school administrators take well-publicized steps to prevent stranger rape by setting up emergency telephone systems and organizing escorts for students who need to walk across campus at night. But stranger rape is actually quite rare on college campuses. When it comes to dealing with the much more common problem of date rape, the administrators are reluctant to get involved. Because the accused rapist is likely to be a fellow student, date rapes create a conflict of interest with party schools' prime mission: retention. If too many rapes are reported on the federal crime forms, party schools risk developing a public reputation as a high rape campus, shunned by fathers of daughters. If they can discourage rape victims from filing official charges, however, they can cover up the number of rapes that actually occur.

By failing to prosecute student rapists, however, party schools are declaring open season on their women students. Men who think they can get away with rape, particularly campus leaders and student athletes, are much more likely to take advantage of a woman, particularly if she is intoxicated. When party schools decline to prosecute rape complaints and post ridiculously low numbers of rapes on their campus crime reports, they are making the problem worse. Women students who assume that rapes are not common have no idea how much danger they are in and are unprepared to deal with date rapes when they occur.

Hazing and Gang Rape

Although it is illegal in every state, hazing by fraternities, sports teams, and even student organizations is a common problem. Although much of this activity is hidden from public view, it often gets out of hand and results in injuries and even death to young people who are pledging. Fraternities are, by far, the strangest and most dangerous organizations on today's college campuses. They are regularly busted for activities like gang rape, homicide by alcohol poisoning, drug dealing, and protection rackets and their missions include the spread of sexism, homophobia, and racism. In other words, they represent the very opposite of the enlightened wisdom that colleges used to provide. Their presence on college campuses is like finding hit men in the Boy Scouts.

Party schools and fraternities exist in one of those symbiotic relationships that are so common at party schools. They need each other to survive. In exchange for allowing fraternities to get a little out of control every once in a while, party school administrators depend on the Greek system to provide the kinds of illegal drinking parties that are an important part of the party school culture. High school students looking for a place to party for five years rightly see the presence of fraternities as an indication that the school is not entirely serious about academics and understands what students are really looking for.

Although many fraternities devolved from the eating clubs and academic organizations of a century ago, they operate today as the outlaw street gangs of academia, complete with deadly initiation rituals and utter disregard for the law. The gangsta culture of the twenty-first century has reinvented fraternities as powerful anti-administration forces to protect the campus party culture and keep it supplied with alcohol, illegal drugs, and places to party. When colleges ban them, they simply move off campus, where the little control that colleges had over them disappears entirely.

Such was the case with the PIGS fraternity at the State University of New York at Geneseo, which operated as an off-campus drinking club after it was disaffiliated by the college in 1996 after two students were hospitalized for alcohol poisoning. The PIGS house was raided regularly by police for supplying minors with alcohol and college officials warned students about associating with it. That was the state of affairs in the spring of 2009 when Arman Partamian, a nineteen-year-old sophomore from Queens, New York, asked to join.

Partamian was a model student, bright and promising, a biology major who worked as a volunteer EMT in the Geneseo area. The fact that someone like him could be drawn to pledge a fraternity like the PIGS should be a warning to every parent: this could have been your son. Adolescent students who are not yet capable of making adult decisions are easy prey for sadistic fraternities looking for victims. Partamian took part in a three-day hazing ritual that culminated on February 28, 2009, when he drank beer, champagne, and vodka before going to the PIGS house, where he was seen with two other pledges jumping over a bonfire in a drunken state. Witnesses said the pledges were being forced to drink entire bottles of liquor at a time.

Partamian was found by paramedics in an upstairs bedroom at 11:00 A.M. the next day and was pronounced dead a short time later. During an autopsy, his blood alcohol level was measured at 0.55, nearly seven times the legal limit. Three members of the PIGS fraternity, including two of Partamian's fellow students, were charged with criminally negligent homicide, as well as unlawfully dealing with an underage drinker and hazing. One of the fraternity members was also charged with evidence tampering after he allegedly removed Partamian's pledge shirt after his death.[129]

Death by fraternity has become increasingly common on college campuses in recent years. Just a few months before Partamian's death, Johnny Smith, an eighteen-year-old freshman at Wabash College in Indiana, died of alcohol poisoning at the Delta Tau Delta fraternity house. Just a few weeks after Partamian's death, Jason Wren, nineteen, a high school honors student, died at the University of Kansas's Sigma Alpha Epsilon fraternity house, where he had consumed ten to twelve beers and was seen drinking from a bottle of Jack Daniel's.[130]

"These deaths, at least several dozen every year, are the end result of decades of collusion between fraternities, college administrators, and college boards of trustees," said Michele Tolela Myers, former president of Sarah Lawrence College. "What they fail to see is that the root of the problem is not simply individual behavior, but the values and norms of the entire fraternity system." Fraternities, she said, should be eliminated from college campuses, just as Williams and Amherst did years before. Until that happens, fraternities will continue their dangerous and illegal behavior and college presidents will have to make "that nightmarish call to parents who won't understand how it was possible that their child was left to die in what they trusted was a safe home away from home."[131]

Party school administrators fail to get tough with fraternities because their alumni are often powerful community leaders and because they are afraid of losing their reputations as party schools, which could drive away the students they need to fill their coffers with tuition money. Fraternity hazing, which can cause death and disfigurement, goes on right in front of the noses of party school administrators, who look the other way to protect the bottom line. Administrators go to seminars and workshops where fraternity practices are discussed in great detail. When they come back, however, they continue to sit on their hands and allow this deadly mischief

to continue because closing fraternities would be a poor marketing decision that could have an impact on their prime directive:
retention.

At New England College in New Hampshire, seven members of
the Sigma Alpha Beta fraternity were charged in March 2009 with
hazing after seven pledges showed up at the college's infirmary with
severe, seven-inch burn marks across their chests where they had
been branded during an initiation ritual. What is unusual in this
case is not that hazing took place but that it was disclosed. Usually, police investigations into hazing are frustrated when everyone
refuses to talk about it.[132]

At Plymouth State College in New Hampshire in 2003, for
example, Kelly Nester, twenty, a pledge with the Sigma Kappa
Omega sorority, died in a car accident a mile from the campus.
Police found that the car contained six blindfolded pledges, but the
code of silence prevented the filing of any charges. Witnesses said
the car was being jerked back and forth on the highway to scare
the pledges when the accident happened. Other common hazing
procedures involve physical and verbal abuse, abandoning pledges
in the woods in winter without clothing, and depriving them of
sleep.[133]

Another common crime committed at fraternity houses is gang
rape. Peggy Reeves Sanday, author of *Fraternity Gang Rape*, said
fraternity brothers refer to it as *gang banging* or *pulling train*, but it
is essentially the same thing. It involves a group of men lining up
like train cars to take turns having sex with the same woman.[134]
There seems to be no documentation on how often this takes place,
because no one, not even the victims, ever discusses it in public,
but estimates range from once a semester to several times a semester
for each fraternity.

My student reporters said the common practice on our campus
was for a fraternity to appoint a member to scout out potential rape
victims on campus. What they looked for were women with low
self-esteem who would not be tempted to report the rape and could

be counted on to keep it secret. The woman was invited to a party only to find she was the only woman there.

Fraternities are, however, only one kind of college group that participates in the sadistic hazing rituals. It is also common among sports teams and even marching bands, but it is hidden from the public, not only by the groups themselves but by administrators concerned about the college's image.

"Spontaneous" Student Riots

Most of the time, party school administrators do an excellent job of preventing the public from getting a good look at what goes on inside their campus walls. But when things get seriously out of control and a campus party turns into a riot, the community quickly finds out how dangerous thousands of intoxicated students can become. The police tend to stay on the sidelines until property damage begins or bonfires set in the middle of the street threaten nearby houses.

At Keene State College, there were dangerous riots when the Red Sox won the World Series in 2004 and 2007. Nearly a thousand students, about one out of five students at the college, started fires, broke windows, turned over cars, threw rocks and bricks at police, and threatened to go on a rampage through the middle of town until they were turned back by dozens of city and state police who had been put on active duty to prevent the riot. Although these seemed to be spontaneous celebrations, my students showed me Facebook groups on which they had been planned weeks in advance. The goal was to create videos of the riot to be posted on YouTube, where you can still view them today.

Police, however, were monitoring the internet site and knew about the students' plans ahead of time. They blocked the college entrances with patrol cars; officers, armed with mace, tear gas, Tasers, and even live ammunition, formed a line around the campus. Alcohol was, of course, the main fuel for the riot, which lasted less than an hour. Estimates of the cost to repair the damage and reimburse the police for overtime were more than $100,000, all of which was billed to the college and ultimately came out of tuition money.

Many of my more responsible students were appalled by this behavior. A columnist for the student newspaper wrote: "How exactly does lighting stuff on fire, littering and smashing car windows constitute celebration?" He called the rioters "moronic," and said it was simply the outlet for something else, "anger and rage fueled by the pent up angst and frustration felt by an entire generation against an establishment that doesn't listen to them."[135]

Many of these sports-based college riots grow out of tailgate parties in the parking lots of sports arenas right under the eyes of campus police, who stand by while thousands of underage students drink out of funnels. At Indiana's three largest public universities, for example, the schools ban alcohol all week, but on game day administrators look the other way, allowing pickup trucks full of beer to drive into the parking lots, a flagrant conflict with the message of moderation that they preach the rest of the time. Some of these students get so drunk in the parking lots that they never make it to the game. Drinking starts at sunrise and lasts late into the afternoon.[136]

A party organized on Facebook in East Lansing, Michigan, near the campus of Michigan State, attracted four thousand students in April 2008. Police in riot gear arrested more than fifty-two people and had to use tear gas to reestablish order. What started with heavy drinking ended with four fires, thrown beer bottles, and arrests for everything from disorderly conduct to felony counts of inciting a riot.[137] Like many of these kinds of riots, there were student film crews on hand to capture the festivities for YouTube.

Partygoers threw beer cans and bottles, women flashed their breasts to the crowd, and signs were torn down. When police arrived, students began to shout "Tear gas us!" But police used smoke grenades and devices that make loud noises and emit bright flashes before they finally granted the students' wishes and used tear gas.

Some students said the party was an attempt to revive Cedar Fest, an annual riot that had been banned for twenty years. When the riot was finally quelled just after 3:00 A.M., the streets were covered in broken glass and trampled lawns were covered in beer.[138]

On the night of April 25, 2009, there were separate riots going on at the same time near college campuses in two states, further demonstrating that these parties are planned events. At Kent State in Ohio, the annual College Fest ended in furniture-fed street fires and police in full riot gear. Witnesses said there were fires fifteen feet high in the middle of the street and students hanging upside down from trees nearby. Police in riot gear used nightsticks and rubber bullet guns to disperse the crowd. After the first fire was put out by firemen, students started three more nearby with two-by-fours torn from interior walls, doors from buildings, and mattresses.[139]

At exactly the same time, students were rioting in Dinkytown, the student ghetto adjacent to the campus of the University of Minnesota in Minneapolis. Students tore down tree limbs and set them on fire in the middle of the street. When students began tipping over parked cars, the police arrived wearing gas masks and spraying pepper spray.[140]

Although students dismiss this kind of behavior as "just letting off a little steam," there is a potential for disaster when thousands of intoxicated students confront armed police in the presence of local property owners who are terrified by what is happening. Party school administrators have to walk a fine line, defending students' rights to have a good time to protect their marketing position and not getting a reputation for being unfriendly to binge drinkers. A common policy is to step in only when the riots spill out into the community and get covered by the news media.

Untreated Mental Illness

This kind of consequence- and responsibility-free culture can have particularly damaging effects on students with behavioral and psychological problems. When they are in high school, these students are required to undergo extensive counseling supervised by parents and school officials who are updated on the students' progress and current state in order to best help them in life and in school. But when they reach the age of eighteen, they are left entirely on their own to manage their own care. Not surprisingly, many of them simply stop taking care of themselves, endangering themselves and those with whom they come in contact.

"Many colleges appear to be more cauldrons of mental perturbation and emotional turmoil than legendary ivory towers," according to an article in *Psychiatric News*. Mark Reed, director of counseling at Dartmouth, said the most common complaint from students was mood disorders, followed by relationship issues involving romantic and family issues. There are also many cases of anxiety disorders, social phobias, eating disorders, and substance abuse. Many of the students he saw had more than one disorder and at his college alone there were fifty students a year taking a leave of absence for psychiatric reasons. As recently as 1996 the number was only eighteen.[141]

Jackie Ayers, director of mental health services at the University of Florida, said the most common disorders there were depression, stress, anxiety, learning disabilities, and psychological trauma as a result of sexual assault.

The National College Health Assessment, published in the spring of 2000, interviewed more than sixteen thousand students at twenty-eight colleges. It found that 10 percent of students had been diagnosed with depression. The U.S. Department of Education reported that between 1999 and 2000, arrests for substance abuse on campus increased by 4 percent, drug arrests were up 10 percent, and murders were up 45 percent.

The number of students with major depression or anxiety disorders has increased sharply during the past five years, according to the October 3, 2001, issue of the *Chronicle of Higher Education*. Morton Silverman, director of student mental health services at the University of Chicago, said most of the mental problems he treated were brought to the college and did not originate while the students were in college.

Richard Kadison, director of mental health services at Harvard, said, "I think there is a general sense that we are seeing much sicker people in college now. We are hospitalizing more people and people are demanding more attentive psychotherapy services."

Incoming freshmen are increasingly arriving at college with bipolar disorders that require five or six medications to keep them stable enough to function, but with no one around to make sure they take their medications, students sometimes forget or take themselves off their meds, resulting in campus incidents that endanger innocent students.

Once again, the law that assumes that anyone who reaches the age of eighteen is an adult vastly overestimates the maturity of college students. Students who depended on their parents to make sure they took their medications and to look after every aspect of their lives were often helpless without them. College policies designed to protect privacy prevent the college from contacting parents or teachers, who have no idea which of the students in class are a potential risk to themselves and others.

Keeping a psychiatric disorder under control in the all-night drinking and partying environment of a college campus can be a challenge for even the most motivated students. Separation from parents, which is difficult for many students, can be much harder for these students.

In some cases, the environment appears to exacerbate, or even actually cause, psychiatric problems. In Alan R. DeSantis's 2007 study of Greek life, he found the interesting phenomenon of women starving themselves and taking laxatives to get smaller, while men took steroids and exercised compulsively to get bigger. He found women who took up cigarette smoking as a way of curbing their appetites and who routinely pressed their fingers down their throats to throw up their lunches and dinners. Sorority sisters described how they would stuff themselves at a Chinese buffet, then go into the bathroom together and throw it all up. Then they would head out to the bars.

Eating disorders are among the most common complaints dealt with by college mental health clinics. With access to all of that gourmet food in the dining commons, freshmen women often find themselves gaining fifteen pounds or more and then struggle to get rid of it. Men who are unhappy with the results gained from lifting weights find they can easily obtain steroids and human growth hormone from dealers on campus.

Suicide rates are another ever-growing issue. A study of thirteen thousand Kansas State University students treated at the university counseling center from 1989 to 2001 showed that the number of students suffering from depression had doubled to 41 percent. The percentage of students who were considered suicidal also doubled to 9 percent. A study of students at Big Ten campuses found that the overall suicide rate was 7.5 per 100,000 students, about twice the rate of non-students in the same age group.[142] The American College Health Association's National College Health Assessment, which interviewed ninety-five thousand students at 117 campuses, found that 9 percent of students had seriously considered suicide and one in one hundred attempted it.

I encountered students who had used a razor blade to cut themselves along their arms; when I suggested that they should go to the counseling center, they told me to mind my own business. I also met students who had inserted metal objects such as paperclips and pins under their skins. When I inquired about this practice at the college's counseling center, I was told there was a name for this: self-embedding disorder. Although all colleges have counseling centers, disturbed students can't be compelled to seek treatment. Some schools do have required treatment sessions. At the University of Missouri, for example, if a student attempts suicide, the college mandates four counseling sessions. However, at my school and many others, it is entirely voluntary and many students refuse, endangering not only themselves but their fellow students.[143]

■ ■ ■

Some students are able to negotiate their way through the party school minefield for five years without becoming victims—or perpetrators. Many do not. Administrators are aware of all these problems but do nothing because cracking down on irresponsible behavior might anger the party students they need to pay the bills. Even when students die of alcohol abuse, the party goes on, endangering not just the binge drinkers but every student on campus.

Covering up student misbehavior is a major preoccupation of party school administrators. Allowing students to do whatever they want for five years would not be tolerated by parents or the public if they knew what was taking place, so colleges make sure that they don't find out. The next chapter will detail the drastic steps that party school administrators take to make sure the public stays in the dark about what really goes on behind the college gates.

An Obsession
with Secrecy

When Jay Wren sent his nineteen-year-old son Jason off to the University of Kansas in August 2008, it was with some mixed emotions. Although he was proud that his son, a popular honor student and defensive back on the Arapahoe High School football team, had been admitted to his college of first choice, he was also worried about his son's safety. Jason's pattern of binge drinking in his hometown of Littleton, Colorado, had led to run-ins with the police and his father was worried that because of its reputation as a party school, KU might turn out to be a danger-ous place to send his son.

Jay Wren called the college regularly that fall, seeking assur-ances that his son was not drinking or getting into trouble. His calls were passed around from office to office, but the answer to his question was always the same. Student disciplinary records are pro-tected by a federal privacy law, he was told. "We'd like to tell you," he was told by college officials, "but our hands are tied. We could lose our federal funding if we broke the law and told you." Jay Wren carefully explained his concerns with each college official he spoke with. All he wanted, he said, was a yes or no answer. Was his son getting into trouble? The only response he received was silence.

What college officials knew but didn't tell Jay Wren was that Jason was already in serious trouble. After getting caught up in the college's binge drinking scene, he was thrown out of his dormitory, Oliver Hall, in the middle of the spring semester. He had been caught twice with alcohol in his room and had refused to participate in an online alcohol education program. When they threw him out of Oliver Hall, the college even prohibited him from visiting his old friends there. They considered him a bad influence and didn't want him associating with the other students. Forced to find a new place to live, Jason talked with his friends at the Sigma Alpha Epsilon fraternity, which like most fraternities had a well-earned reputation as a binge drinker's paradise with parties nearly every night. Jason applied to become a member and was accepted.

A short time later, Jason called his father and admitted he had been kicked out of Oliver Hall but downplayed the violations, saying they amounted to trivial violations like finding a glass in his dorm room and holding a beer for a friend. He said he expected fewer complaints at the fraternity house where he would now live. After that phone call, Jay Wren thought about all he had heard about college fraternity houses and decided it was time to pull his son out of KU before it was too late. It turned out to be the last conversation Jay Wren ever had with his son.

The next week, on March 8, Jay Wren received a call from Kansas police telling him that Jason had been found dead in the fraternity house. Police told him that Jason had gone out to dinner with his new fraternity brothers and drank margaritas by the pitcher. When he returned to the fraternity house, he had ten to twelve beers and drank from a bottle of Jack Daniel's. Walking around holding the bottle, Jason bragged that he never got sick when he drank. Shortly after that, he passed out and his brothers took him up to his room and put him to bed. He died sometime during the night, but his body was not discovered until the next afternoon because his brothers thought he was sleeping it off. An autopsy found that, at the time of his death, Jason's blood alcohol level was 0.362, more than four times the state's legal limit for intoxication.

"If they (KU) had let us know all of this, we could have sat down with him," Jay Wren said. "I would have pulled him out of school to get him back here where we could keep an eye on him. We would have made him live at home. . . ."[144]

"One week of fraternity living killed him," said Jay Wren. "I feel cheated that the college put up a barrier between my son and us as parents. These kids are not adults at nineteen. They're not adults at twenty and in some cases they are not even adults at twenty-one. Parents are the ones that care most about them and somehow [college administrators] interpret a law where we're excluded."

Jay Wren finally got his son's disciplinary records a few weeks after Jason's death, but the college remained steadfast in maintaining that it had done nothing wrong. The death had occurred off campus, out of the college's control, explained Marlesa Roney, KU's vice provost for student success. "There is no evidence that parental notification makes any difference," she told the Associated Press.[145] Jay Wren thought that was total hogwash and started a national campaign to force colleges to release disciplinary records to parents.

The story caught the attention of Jim Boyle, president of College Parents of America, an advocacy group, who said that although privacy rules differed from college to college, they should err on the side of providing more information, not less. "I believe they should use their interpretation to better inform parents about their son or daughter, and not use (privacy laws) as an excuse to withhold information."[146]

But it took the death of another KU student a few weeks later before KU was finally forced to look into its policy of keeping parents in the dark about disciplinary rules. Dalton Eli Hawkins fell off a college building roof while he was drunk. Local newspapers began to question KU's policy and began asking a lot of very embarrassing questions about how well party schools like KU take care of their students. Finally, in May, two months after Jason's death, KU announced a new policy. Parents will now be notified about all drinking violations, including underage drinking. But it was too late for Jason Wren, Dalton Hawkins, and the other 1,698 college students who die each year while drunk. Hundreds of other party schools—along with many elite schools—around the country continue to abuse privacy laws by refusing to notify parents of even the most drastic disciplinary violations.

The Code of Silence

When parents drop their children off on campus at the beginning of freshman year, most don't realize they are also giving up something else: the personal contact with teachers and administrators that they enjoyed when their children were in high school. Parents who had been encouraged to engage in friendly and helpful chats with teachers and counselors and to share information to help with their children's problems are simply not ready when party schools slam the door in their faces and refuse to disclose any information about their children.

In high school, when something goes wrong at school, parents are called the same day and informed in detail about the problem and what can be done about it. Parents and teachers meet often to discuss children's progress and come up with an individual education plan to make the best possible choices to ensure educational success. If Johnny doesn't show up for school, the principal calls the parents to find out why. If Johnny is sent to detention for not doing his homework, the parents are informed. Working in tandem, parents and educators can keep pretty close tabs on children; although it doesn't always cure the problems, it nearly always works in the students' favor.

In college, particularly at party schools, however, the situation is the exact opposite. Parents are deliberately pushed out of the picture. Party school administrators argue that their students, nearly all of whom are over the age of eighteen, are legally adults and should be allowed to make their own decisions. The laws in most states also set eighteen as the age when adolescents become adults. In many cases, like that of Jason Wren, that turns out to be a disastrous assumption. Although a minority of college students are mature enough to make responsible decisions, most of them, left on their own, make incredibly poor and sometimes deadly decisions. They drink themselves into unconsciousness. They have unsafe sex with strangers. They stay up all night and sleep through their classes. They ignore their own safety by taking dangerous risks. They abuse drugs. They take out unnecessary loans or use credit cards to go on spring break in Cancun. Clearly, the majority of party school students still need the kind of direction and guidance they received in high school from parents, teachers, and counselors.

Party school administrators, more than anyone else, are aware of all this immature student behavior, so why don't they invite parents to help? Although they use the privacy laws as an excuse, the real reason is that party school administrators think of parents as troublemakers who should simply pay the bills and stay out of the way. If parents were more involved in their children's lives in college, it would create lots of problems for administrators, who often speak of them derogatorily as "helicopter parents," reluctant to let their children go. Parents would likely question the wisdom of inflating grades, dumbing down classes, moving back the class drop date, and reducing the number of classes required for graduation. Parents would insist the college protect their children from the hazards of campus life, out-of-control binge drinking, and the lax enforcement of rape laws.

When parents call the college to talk with a teacher or a counselor, they are turned away with the same dismissive explanation that Jay Wren received. My faculty handbook warned that it was a "serious violation of federal law" to say anything at all to parents. All calls were to be forwarded to the administration. Parents are never informed of anything that happens to their children on campus, no matter how dangerous it is.

The results have been tragic. College students can be arrested for felonies like assault, arson, or robbery, or be treated for depression and suicide attempts; they can flunk multiple classes, fail to show up for classes for months, and go through the college disciplinary process over and over without a single word being said to parents. Students can be raped, assaulted, or stalked and the parents are never informed. When students exhibit suicidal behaviors, for example, or when they are addicted to drugs or alcohol, elaborate procedures are in place to deal with these problems. Often, multiple counselors and health-care workers are aware of the problems over a period of years. For parents, however, the first notice that anything is wrong is delayed until the college president calls to let them know that their son or daughter is dead.

Colleges use the same process when news reporters show up and request information about campus crimes, average grades, mental health statistics, and other information that the public has a right to know. The excuse that party school administrators use is the same one that Jay Wren received over and over. It's all because of a federal privacy law called the Family Educational Rights and Privacy Act, which administrators call FERPA (pronounced FUR-pa).

The Strange History of FERPA

What was Congress thinking when it passed such an outrageously irresponsible law as FERPA? The answer, surprisingly, is that the original law was intended to protect parents' access to student records, not restrict it. The law as originally drawn didn't apply to college students at all. The intent was to protect parents' rights to examine all their children's elementary and secondary school records (including grades, disciplinary records, and assessment tests) so they could be more involved in their children's educations.

Just before the law was passed in 1974, however, someone noticed that the law could be interpreted to include college students as well, so a last-minute amendment was added specifying that the law applied only to students under the age of eighteen. Once the child became eighteen, the amendment said, access to educational records was limited to the student. This was supposed to protect the privacy of college students from examination by anyone outside the college; no one thought that they might be locking out parental access to the records. It was this last-minute, poorly-thought-out change that caused trouble then and is still causing trouble today.

Because it was so hastily written, the law began causing no end of confusion about what should and should not be made public and to whom even before it went into effect in 1975. The Health, Education, and Welfare Department, which was supposed to enforce the law, had not been able to draw up regulations for the law's enforcement and there were reports of arguments within the department about how to interpret the law. Those disputes have continued for more than forty years and resulted in a number of battles in federal court over what the law actually means. It was no small matter because the law required HEW to cut federal funding for schools that violated the laws.

During the late 1970s, however, college administrators gradually discovered what a fantastic gift Congress had bestowed upon them. It allowed them to draw a cloak of secrecy over nearly every aspect of their operations. Those annoying parents and those nosy journalists could be safety locked out so the education professionals could do their work in private with no one looking over their shoulders and second-guessing them. Party schools expanded the scope of the law beyond anything anyone had ever imagined by declaring that all of the college's records were "education records," not just grades, and access to any of them was denied by the law. Administrators used the law to protect themselves from every kind of inquiry, even requests made under the federal and state freedom of information laws. They stopped sending grade reports to parents. They stopped notifying parents of disciplinary actions, including arrests for felonies. Party schools found they could chase annoying parents like Jay Wren away and not have to deal with their complaints and questions about school policies.

The college judicial boards, some of which were once open to the public, were tightly locked down so no one could find out how many students were disciplined or expelled or even the charges against them. This locked out the press, which used to ask embarrassing questions about what went on inside the college walls. Now, party schools could dismiss reporters' questions with the catch-all excuse, "Sorry, federal law prevents us from talking about that." The only time outsiders got a look behind the cloak of invisibility was when students did things that were impossible to cover up, like murder, arson, and suicide.

Over the past forty years, federal courts have ruled repeatedly that party school administrators' broad interpretation of FERPA was incorrect. It went way beyond what Congress intended, and Congress itself modified the law twice, beginning in the 1990s, to make its intentions more clear. The law, Congress said, did not apply to disciplinary records but to a narrowly defined group of "education records" like grades. To this day, however, colleges continue to use their own, and clearly incorrect, interpretation of the law that nearly everything the college does is secret.

When parents like Jay Wren run up against FERPA, few of them understand what a paper tiger it is. What Jay Wren did not know was that FERPA does not apply to the kinds of student disciplinary records he was seeking. This has been made clear by Congress, the Department of Education, and court rulings. When parents call, administrators are free to discuss student disciplinary actions with them. Party schools, however, have insisted on their own broad and clearly incorrect interpretation in order to keep those outside the college from prying too deeply into the inconvenient truths about what goes on at party schools. KU also didn't tell Jay Wren that he could have had Jason sign a release form that would have allowed Jay access to the records he sought. KU didn't tell Jay Wren that FERPA has such a low priority at the U.S. Department of Education that it has never been enforced, not once, in forty-five years.[147]

In May 2009, a Columbus, Ohio, newspaper investigated why there was such a difference among college sports teams about the kinds of information that were made public.[148] Some colleges released almost everything and other colleges released nearly nothing. Reporters found that most colleges that refused to disclose information cited FERPA as the reason. But when the newspaper asked James Buckley, the former New York senator who originally wrote the FERPA law, he was stunned. It was never his intention to prevent colleges from disclosing disciplinary information, said Buckley, who is now a federal judge in Connecticut. He said colleges were obviously misinterpreting the law and planned to urge Congress to amend the law back to his original intention: to protect parental access to school records through the entire educational process, not to restrict them.

Why the Report Card Never Arrives

How much of a difference does parental access to these records make? Sometimes a lot. A generation ago, parents who were concerned about how well their children were doing in college could look forward to receiving a computer printout containing their children's grades from the previous semester. After spending all that money, parents think they should at least have that much feedback about how their children are doing. And parents who are financially supporting their child, when they know what's going on, can make a big difference in his or her behavior.

Thanks to FERPA, today's colleges never send grade reports to parents. Information about test scores, assignment scores, and even final grade reports are closely held secrets. In fact, most colleges have done away with printed grade reports entirely, replacing them with information on websites protected by passwords.

Grade reports have been off-limits to parents since FERPA went into effect in 1975, but as long as colleges sent grade reports to students' home addresses, most parents didn't mind opening the letter from the college and taking a look. It was only when colleges went to computer-only reports that parents began to feel left out of the loop entirely. Like other aspects of the FERPA law, students can sign a waiver allowing their parents access to the reports. Or students can simply give parents the password to the college website. The colleges, of course, usually don't tell parents about these options, but parents who are informed about them can put some pressure on their children to surrender the information.

Parents who do, however, hit another snag. Because, as explained in a previous chapter, most colleges inflate grades to the extent that no one receives anything lower than a B, the reports are often misleading for parents. Usually, most of the students get an A and the lower 30 to 50 percent get a B. Parents who still believe that a B means *good* need to understand that at today's colleges it means just the opposite: *below average*.

Preventing parents from looking at their children's academic records creates a number of serious problems. Students can drop out of school or stop going to classes and parents aren't given a single clue about what is going on if the student refuses to tell them. Many parents, accustomed to being called by high schools when something goes wrong, interpret the silence as reassurance that everything is going fine. Eventually, the student might reveal that he decided not to attend classes at all for a particular semester or was convicted of a crime by a campus judicial board and expelled, but they won't hear any of that from the school.

On one occasion, I deliberately broke the FERPA law by making a copy of a disruptive student's Facebook home page and sent it anonymously to her parents. The page featured a photo of the student kneeling down with a hose in her mouth while her friends poured a bottle of vodka into a funnel attached to the other end of the hose. A week later, the page had been removed and, although she had dropped my class, another of her professors said her behavior had radically improved. This indicated to me how different college would be if professors could simply write notes to parents updating them on their children's behavior. It works so much better in secondary schools. But as long as we have a FERPA law, students will misbehave and parents, who are usually paying the bills, will remain uninformed about what really goes on at school.

Secret Treatments for Mentally Ill Students

FERPA also interferes with colleges' abilities to deal with mentally ill students, often allowing them to go untreated. Parents often have no idea there is a problem until their children kill themselves or attack other students.

Elizabeth Shin, a nineteen-year old sophomore from New Jersey who attended the Massachusetts Institute of Technology, was a smart, talented overachiever and so obsessed with becoming the best in her class that she drove herself to distraction. Her bouts with mental illness began in high school but got worse at MIT, which was known at the time for the pressure it put on students to succeed.

She was treated numerous times for depression at the college's mental health clinic after a suicide attempt and one of the doctors who examined her had considered hospitalizing her. A number of MIT administrators were familiar with her problem, as were several counselors. Even her friends were aware of her several attempted suicides. The only people who did not know were her parents.

When her parents visited her in her dorm room on April 13, 2000, they had no idea that the night before Elizabeth had held a knife to her chest but had not been able to make the final thrust to kill herself. To her parents, she seemed a little stressed out but no more than usual. They felt there was no reason to be concerned.

The next night, she set herself on fire in her room and firemen had to break down the door in an attempt to rescue her. That night, her parents received a phone call from Cambridge, notifying them that their daughter had been in a fire. She died a few days later and it was only at that point that the college told them about Elizabeth's long series of treatments for mental illness. They were also told that a dozen other MIT students had committed suicide over the past decade. At MIT, the number of student visits to counseling centers jumped 63 percent between 1995 and 2000. They also found that suicide is the second leading cause of death for college students in the United States.

When the Shins asked the college why they had not been informed about any of this before their daughter's death, they were told about the FERPA law. When the Shins talked with their daughter's friends and teachers, they all seemed to know about Elizabeth's suicide attempts.

"We know about privacy laws and we respect them," said Elizabeth's mother, Kisuk Shin. "But this was a life-or-death situation. They told us Elizabeth didn't want us to know." Her father, Cho Shin, said, "If they let us know, just the one phone call, she would be alive right now."[149]

When the Shins filed a lawsuit for wrongful death, MIT claimed there was evidence of mental illness and depression dating back to Shin's high school years, so the dispute became one of who knew what and when. The school argued that the parents had passed up opportunities to have Shin examined and they should have been able to read the signs as well. Since her death, MIT has begun a suicide prevention program that includes parents whenever it can. "Part of the treatment plan is to engage the family," said Allen Siegel, head of the MIT counseling center. "We make it clear to the student that is how you get better."[150] MIT's practice, however, is not common. The gulf that opens up between parents and students after they head off to college is magnified by the FERPA law, which makes nearly every aspect of a student's college life secret.

"It's tricky because the kid is an adult," said Dr. David A. Brent, a professor of psychiatry at the University of Pittsburgh School of Medicine. "If a child doesn't want them to contact the parent, then you're in a very difficult situation. It highlights the stress on colleges to be 'in loco parentis' to the child, even though they may not want to be."[151]

"It's really frightening," said Nancy Paetzold, a New Jersey anesthesiologist, whose son Jeremy took his own life several years ago. "You pay $35,000 and you can't even get to find out what your kid went to student health for. Somehow there has to be feedback. They're your kids and you don't get a second chance."[152]

The most famous failure of the FERPA law, however, is the case of Seung-Hui Cho, the Virginia Tech student who murdered thirty-two people and wounded twenty-five others during a day-long rampage on April 16, 2007. He had been treated for various mental illnesses including anxiety and speech impediments dating back to elementary school and had been prescribed medications to treat them. Although his high school had files full of information about him, the high school was prevented from passing this on to Virginia Tech by—you guessed it—the FERPA law.[153]

A number of professors ordered Cho removed from their classes because they found him menacing. He wore sunglasses all the time. He would climb under the desks and take photographs of women's legs and would write violent and obscene poetry. Linda Roy, the college's director of creative writing, sent letters about him to numerous administrators, but they replied there was nothing they could do unless he threatened to harm himself or others. Under the terms of the FERPA law, it is illegal for professors to get together and discuss information about students, a common practice in secondary schools. If this had been allowed to take place, perhaps the college would have been able to take some kind of action to obtain help for Cho.

Roy attempted to work with Cho on a one-on-one basis but became alarmed by his behavior and suggested that he seek counseling, but no one ever followed up on this request. Students observed him riding his bicycle in circles for hours, listening to the same song on the CD player over and over, or staring out the window. He had been charged several times with stalking women students.

On December 13, 2005, he was found to be mentally ill and in need of hospitalization by a mental health clinic, which declared him an immediate danger to himself and others, but a judge overruled this recommendation and he was treated as an outpatient. Although his family attempted to help him while he was in high school, once he went to college, they lost their legal authority over him and, thanks to Virginia Tech's interpretation of the FERPA law, the college refused to inform them about what was going on.

His mental status did not disqualify him from purchasing guns in Virginia and he was able to purchase weapons legally on eBay. During the subsequent investigation, Virginia Tech, using the FERPA law, refused to surrender Cho's medical records, even though he was now dead. They were not released until his family signed a release.

In the final report on the case, Virginia Tech was cited for failure to "connect the dots" and for not taking action to ensure Cho received proper treatment. The college was also cited for "incorrect interpretation of privacy laws."

In 2009, a follow-up state report found that Virginia Tech waited an hour and a half between the time it first learned about the massacre and when it officially locked down the campus and informed students and officials. During those crucial ninety minutes, administrators locked down their own offices and warned their own families. Why the hesitation? It should come as no surprise that administrators were more concerned about bad publicity than they were about student safety. When administrators were first informed that there was a "gunman on the loose," they added the message "this is not releaseable yet." During those ninety minutes, an administrator sent out this message to other administrators: "Just try to make sure it doesn't get out."[154]

In reaction to the Virginia Tech shootings, the U.S. Department of Education issued a 289-page guide in December 2008 designed to help colleges determine what they could and could not make public and when they could call in parents to help. The idea that FERPA prevented faculty and staff from sharing information on troubled students, the report said, was in error. Under the new rules, colleges may disclose information about someone "if there is a significant threat to the health or safety of the student or other individuals."[155]

The Destruction of Campus Discourse

FERPA's effects are felt not only in the kind of tragedies that end in death, but in daily campus interaction. To understand the ridiculous muzzle that FERPA creates during ordinary discussions, I would like to relate a telephone conversation I had one day with the director of the campus student center.

> DSC: A student has complained to me about an interaction you recently had with her.
> ME: What about?
> DSC I can't tell you. It's confidential.
> ME: So who was it who complained?
> DSC: I can't tell you. It's confidential.
> ME: So what do you expect me to do?
> DSC: I thought you should know.

I mentioned this to my department chair, who called the student center director and got the very same runaround. It took several days for the director to contact the student so the director could be "released from confidentiality commitments." It was only then that I learned the student had complained because I had reprimanded her for holding a meeting that I had scheduled a half hour early so that I was unable to attend. Over and over, simple problems go unresolved because of these kinds of ridiculous restrictions on what can be discussed.

How Party Schools Deliberately Cover Up Campus Crimes

Party schools routinely and blatantly abuse the FERPA law to cover up crimes committed on college campuses, even though federal law requires them to disclose crime statistics to the public. Hiding behind FERPA's confidentiality rules allows college administrators to create a false image that their colleges are free from the kinds of problems one would expect when five thousand to twenty thousand adolescents, many of them consistently intoxicated, converge on a few acres of ground. For years, colleges, citing FERPA, refused to release any statistics or police reports of serious crimes. Although they said this was to protect confidentiality, it's no secret that the real reason was to protect themselves from the bad publicity generated by high profile crimes like rape, arson, and assault.

Party schools' broad interpretation of the FERPA law allows them to conduct their own secret criminal justice system out of sight of the public, parents, and the press. These campus judicial boards have a long history on college campuses, but the FERPA law allows them to continue in secrecy when nearly every other kind of official hearing board has been opened up by federal and state freedom of information laws. The municipal police and public prosecutors are not even aware that crimes have been committed. Party school administrators act as investigator, judge, prosecutor, defense attorney, and jury all at the same time.

Because preventing bad publicity is one of college officials' primary interests, all of these actions have conflicts of interest. The college's reputation always comes first and justice takes a back seat. In a 2004 press release, the watchdog group Security of Campus charged that college judicial boards abuse the FERPA law to operate "Star Chamber" courts, "which hand down relatively light sentences such as 500-word essays or short suspensions from school for serious crimes such as arson, assault, and rape."[156] Although the public might think these boards handle only minor violations of campus rules like plagiarism or sneaking into a concert without a ticket, the reality is that they deal with major felonies. Their rules are secret. Their proceedings are secret and the results are secret. Critics point out that they are run more like the Gestapo than anything resembling an American court proceeding and, like any other secret organization, they are subject to abuse.

College judicial boards routinely require rape victims to sign confidentiality agreements before they can be told the results of a disciplinary action. The purpose of these agreements is, once again, to prevent the bad publicity that party school administrators seek to avoid at all costs. In a 2004 ruling against Georgetown University, the U.S. Department of Education ruled that federal law protected victims' right to be told about how the case was resolved without signing the confidentiality agreements.

A rape victim, Kate Dieringer, signed a confidentiality agreement and found out that the man she accused had been expelled from school. Later, however, he appealed and had his sentence reduced to a one-year suspension. When she attempted to complain about the reduction of the sentence, the college barred her from filing a complaint because of the confidentiality agreement.

"Forcing a victim to sign a confidentiality agreement in order to find out the outcome of a hearing which they initiated is not only against the law, it's inhumane," Dieringer said. S. Daniel Carter, senior vice president of Security on Campus, said the Department of Education ruling "breaks the culture of silence that campus rape thrives in."[157]

In celebrating this decision, Security on Campus called it a victory for advocates of safety on campus. "This ruling ensures that rape victims won't be silenced by schools which are more concerned about their image than keeping their students safe," the group announced.[158] "If they want to talk to their friends about what happened to them, they can. If they want to tell them who did it, they can. . . . If they want to hold a news conference and announce to the campus just how the school handled the case, they can. If doing this will help them heal, then they should do just that, and the school can't stop them."[159]

But the secret court system continues to be used by administrators at colleges across the country because it serves their interests to pretend that campuses are safe when most of them are actually high crime areas. These courts exist in a kind of parallel judicial universe where serious offenses, which would attract negative media attention, are disposed of discreetly under the same student conduct codes that forbid plagiarism.[160]

Although college officials say victims can always take their cases to the outside courts, outside prosecutors complain that the campus systems undermine their cases before they can get them. Colleges' prime interests in the system are to protect their own people, including star athletes, athletic departments, fraternities, and local businesses that benefit from the college drinking culture.[161]

R. Keegan Federal, an Atlanta lawyer who challenged and won a case against the University of Georgia's judicial system, said the systems avoided any kind of accountability. "What we've got here," he said, "is people across the whole United States, people who are selected by a process we don't know about and sit on hearings that are secret and make decisions affecting people's lives and freedom and careers, and yet nobody knows about it. Frankly, it scares the hell out of you when you read some of these things."[162]

Jeffrey Newman, a lawyer for Security on Campus, said judicial boards usually have conflicts of interest because their sense of justice is always tempered by the absolute necessity of protecting the college from bad publicity, a concern that never enters into cases in the regular judicial system.

Miami University in Ohio reported a "zero" in the rape column in its official crime report for 1995. That seemed a little low for a campus with sixteen thousand students, so a *New York Times* reporter looked a little further and found that two rapes of students had been reported to the local police, but the college did not count them because they were off campus, just blocks from the campus gates. The reporter also identified twenty-one additional rapes that had been reported to various campus agencies but not to the campus police. One rape victim told the reporter that the college's judicial affairs coordinator suggested to her that, instead of going after the rapist, she handle the case through mediation as a "misunderstanding." When she declined, a formal hearing was begun. It lasted twenty minutes and it found the rapist guilty of sexual assault. When the victim asked the next day what the punishment would be, she was told by college officials that they could not tell her—FERPA law, of course. What they did not tell her was that three years earlier the U.S. Department of Education had specifically ruled that rape victims have a right to know the punishments handed out to rapists. When the victim's father complained, the college told him that the rapist had been sentenced to a "student conduct probation."[163]

The Clery Act and Unreported Statistics

Incorrect FERPA interpretation allowed colleges to cover up the high rates of crime from 1975 until 1986, when a brutal murder shook the entire system to the core. Jeanne Clery, a freshman at Lehigh University in Pennsylvania, was tortured, raped, sodomized, and murdered in her dorm room during the early morning of April 5, 1986. Her killer, a fellow student she had never met, was a campus drug and alcohol abuser who gained access to her dormitory room when fellow students had propped open doors that should have been locked. Although most parents would have simply buried their daughter and shared their grief, Connie and Howard Clery demanded answers and finally got them.

"We learned that institutional response to such tragedies could involve callousness, coverups, and stonewalling," wrote Howard Clery. "Lehigh officials publicly passed off Jeanne's torturer/

murderer as an aberration. The college, in an ill-conceived attempt to protect its image, produced a self-serving report written by one of its trustees." The report said the college's safety policies were adequate, but Clery discovered that there had been 181 reports of propped-open doors in Jeanne's dormitory during the previous four months.[164]

"We learned that crime on campus was one of the best-kept secrets in the country," Clery continued. "We learned that the true picture of campus crime is startling, even horrifying." In 1987, he found there were thirty-one murders, more than fifteen hundred armed robberies, and thirteen thousand physical assaults on American campuses. Armed with this information, the Clerys began a campaign to tear the covers off the campus crime problem. They began with a lawsuit against Lehigh for negligence. When they won, they used the proceeds to set up Security on Campus, the nation's foremost nonprofit campus crime watchdog group.

"Our daughter died because of what she didn't know," said Clery. To ensure that other students did not fall victim to a false sense of security, his group began lobbying state and federal government officials to enact laws that required colleges to make their crime statistics public. In 1990, Congress passed the Jeanne Clery Act, which modified FERPA to require all colleges receiving federal funds to collect accurate information about campus crime and make it available to the public. The idea, Clery said, was that awareness that they live in a high crime area can prevent students from becoming victims.

The act is pretty straightforward and should have helped students choose a safe campus, but instead of complying with the law, party school administrators have spent nineteen years fighting it and looking for loopholes to avoid compliance. It was another case of party school administrators putting their own self-interest above the safety of their students by lying to the public and covering up serious crimes. As quickly as Congress plugged the loopholes, party school lawyers found other ways to avoid disclosing the truth about crimes. The reason for this is simple. Parents want a safe campus for their children and colleges that accurately report their crime statistics are at a disadvantage compared with colleges that cook the books and report artificially low numbers.[165]

"When universities publish the crime statistics, students only receive half the picture," said Ellen Wilkins, a student at the University of Georgia who is president of Safe Campuses Now.[166] She found that there was a severe loophole that permits colleges to use only the crimes that were committed on campus and ignore the crimes students commit just a few feet from the campus wall. Her group found that of 370 crimes in which Georgia students were the victims, 165 occurred off campus and were therefore not reported.

The crime report for Ohio State in 1994 listed just seven forcible sex offenses, but Carin Quirke, head of Women Against Rape in Columbus, said her organization hears complaints from seven Ohio State students a month. Tina Thome, a graduate student who works in the university's Rape Education and Prevention Program, said her office regularly talked with victims of rapes that were not reported to campus police. Ron Michalec, the chief of campus police at Ohio State, admitted that he only reported rapes in which victims filed an official complaint and many sex-offense victims choose not to file an official report. If they "don't want a report, I don't report it," he said.[167]

According to the U.S. Department of Justice, only 37 percent of colleges report crimes in a way that is consistent with the intent of the Clery law. Although colleges insist that the problem is with the definition of terms like *student* and *campus*, the real reason is that party school administrators are deliberately cooking the books to compete with other colleges in terms of safety. There is a clear conflict of interest here. Although the law requires colleges to report crimes, it's in the colleges' best interest to cover them up.[168]

As recently as June 2008, Eastern Michigan University was fined $350,000 for failure to comply with the Clery Act. Their offense? The college tried to cover up the murder of student Laura Dickinson and did not notify the campus community, as required by the Clery law. After an investigation, three top college officials departed, including president John Fallon, who was fired. The college also paid a $2.5 million settlement to the family of the victim.[169]

As quickly as party school lawyers can find loopholes in the law that will allow them to cover up crimes, Security on Campus lobbies Congress to revise the law to cover its original and simple intention: all crimes have to be publicly disclosed. This cat-and-mouse game continues to this day, despite the fact that allowing students to think their campuses are safer than they actually are encourages students to be unprepared to be a victim and to take unnecessary chances.

While I was advisor to the student newspaper at Keene State College in New Hampshire, my student reporters ran into this all the time. Rape victims who came forward and wanted the newspaper to write about what happened to them said they had filed a report, but the campus police insisted that no report had been filed. Similarly, students who had items taken from their dorm rooms were told that the crime could not be officially investigated unless they had the serial number of the item, which, of course, they usually did not have. Real police would never require this kind of thing. Crimes that my student reporters had witnessed and wished to write about did not show up on the official weekly crime logs and, as far as the college was concerned, they did not happen.

At Franklin Pierce University in early January 2009, the local town police were attempting to investigate a string of burglaries on the campus but were thwarted by the campus safety officers, who had destroyed most of the evidence by not sealing the crime scene. This conflict, which appeared on the front page of the local newspaper, is easy to explain if you understand that the mission of the town police is to investigate crimes and solve them, but the mission of the campus police at party school campuses is to cover them up.

In New York State, an investigation by the state comptroller's office in 2008 found that two-thirds of the campuses of the State

University of New York were keeping two sets of books on campus crime. One was the official one sent off to Washington to comply with the Clery law requirements. The other, for internal use only, contained the real numbers, which were a lot higher. The investigation also found that colleges were failing to report serious crimes such as sexual offenses, burglaries, and drug offenses.[170]

"Safety has to come first on college campuses," said State Comptroller Thomas P. DiNapoli. "Parents and students have a right to know, and colleges have a responsibility to report. Accuracy is the key and some SUNY schools have been inaccurately reporting serious crimes on campus. Not telling the full story on crime will not make crime disappear. What we found is disturbing and must be addressed. Students should have a clear and accurate picture of what's happening on their campus so they can protect themselves and their property."

Auditors found that nineteen of SUNY's twenty-nine colleges had underreported their crime statistics. Nine schools underreported more than twenty crimes. Three campuses—Oneonta, Delhi, and Cobleskill—had more than forty crimes that were not on the federal report. SUNY Stony Brook underreported its campus crimes by nearly 50 percent on its 2006 report, including thirty-three burglaries. The college was able to do this by misclassifying the burglaries as larcenies, which do not have to be reported. In nine separate incidents, campus police classified on-campus sexual offenses as investigations and did not include the nature of the crimes. The University at Buffalo failed to report seventeen drug offenses and underreported seventy-five disciplinary actions, violations of law that did not result in arrests, including forty-three drug violations, twenty-seven liquor violations, and five weapons incidents.

Officials at the schools gave a whole range of explanations for the discrepancies, including lack of training, computer malfunctions, and lack of manpower. However, in every single case, the errors resulted in underreporting of crimes. There was never an error that resulting in overreporting of crime. It's easy to see what is going on here: deliberate distortion by party schools to protect themselves from bad publicity and to protect their marketing position, exactly what corporate executives are trained to do.

Why the News Media Ignores the Problem

If all of this bad news about how dangerous college campuses are comes as a surprise to you, there's a very good reason. The American news media has largely ignored the problems created when administrators whose first priority used to be education were replaced with administrators with their eyes focused on the bottom line. Reporters attempting to do serious stories about problems on college campuses are repeatedly turned away when the college cites the FERPA law. Reporters rely on college public relations departments who pitch them stories about the 10 percent of engaged and excellent students and play down the news of students who are arrested for drug dealing, public intoxication, rioting, sexual abuse, and assault. News about how little college graduates actually know is relegated to Jay Leno's late night "Jaywalking" segments, during which he interviews students who think the Eiffel Tower is in London or that the United States never declared war against Japan.

"Higher education's weaknesses and shortcomings remain largely out of sight to reporters," said Gene I. Maeroff, a former national education reporter for the *New York Times* and now a senior fellow at the Hechinger Institute on Education and the Media at Columbia. "Higher education is Teflon-coated, remarkably immune to criticism." When reporters visit college campuses, they are there to report on sports, tuition increases, and admissions numbers. Everything else seems to be off-limits.[171]

"Americans remain relatively uninformed about the state of quality in the academy," he said. Students and their parents should demand of higher education the same kinds of consumer information they demand about health care, sport utility vehicles, or prescription drugs. Instead, they seem to accept blindly that colleges are delivering a quality product with little evidence on which to base that opinion. The steady decline in academic standards and expectations and the inflation of grades remains largely invisible to them.

Jay Mathews, education reporter and columnist for the *Washington Post*, said academia's claims about the quality of their product go largely unexamined. "Those groups that do measure the weight of an undergraduate education do it quietly, and often decline to disclose their findings without the permission of the universities that would prefer to keep their failings to themselves," he said.[172]

Exposing what really goes on inside the gates of party schools seems not to be on the news media's agenda, despite all the evidence documented in professional journals and the anecdotal evidence of individual students, who only become newsworthy when they shoot people or are arrested for a sensational crime.

Mark D. Soskin, associate professor of economics at the University of Central Florida, said that if parents and state legislators were aware of the decline in standards at American colleges, there would be a loud uproar of protest and a resistance from parents when it came time to pay those expensive tuition bills. It would soon be evident, he said that "the emperor, if not naked, had a much skimpier wardrobe than commonly presumed." It's convenient for everyone involved to pretend that high quality and relevant learning is going on, and students, faculty, taxpayers, legislators, alums, and donors have informally conspired to look the other way.[173]

Parents and state legislators seem to accept on faith that whatever course of study students pursue in college will teach them what they need to know for today's competitive and complex environment, said Carol G. Schneider, president of the Association of American Colleges and Universities. "But in practice, college figures in the public imagination as something of a magical mystery tour. It is important to be admitted; it is also important to graduate with a degree. But what one does in between, what students actually learn in college, is largely unknown and largely unchallenged."[174]

Campus Journalists Denied Information

Among those shut out by party school administrators' refusal to disclose information on campus crimes are the colleges' own student newspapers. As a student newspaper advisor for a dozen years, I faced this problem about once a month when my reporters told me that the college was refusing to provide information that they had every right to access. This problem only got worse when the college newspaper was posted online so the public and parents everywhere could read it on the internet. I was constantly asked by administrators to "tone down" the content. Not censor it, of course, but just keep students from writing about things that made the college look bad.

Despite being amateurs, my student reporters dug up all kinds of embarrassing stories: students forced to stand outside for hours in subzero temperatures to register for dormitory rooms, student residences with mold so bad that students were going to the hospital, and a college daycare playground that was contaminated by lead paint chips falling off a nearby building. The students got away with reporting this because I backed them up. Any censorship, I warned, and my students would take their stories to the *New Hampshire Union Leader*, which would not hesitate to report the news, as well as the campus efforts to censor their own students. You can imagine how popular this made me with my bosses. It turns out, however, that the student press is under attack all over the country for writing truthful articles that damage party schools' marketing position and public relations efforts.

In 1991, student journalists at Southwest Missouri State University asked for campus crime records, but the university denied the request, citing FERPA and its duty to protect students' privacy. Judge Russell G. Clark of the Federal District Court in Missouri ruled that FERPA was never intended to include criminal records and sided with the students.

Traci M. Bauer, the editor of the student newspaper, correctly stated that the real concern was not about students' privacy but about the college's ability to control bad news. "It's the school's image that is being protected," she told the *New York Times*, "and not the privacy of the students."[175] Commenting on the case, Constance Clery, the mother of the victim for which the Clery Act is named, said the ruling gave on-campus crime reports the same status as off-campus reports. "If these crimes occurred off campus the information would be released," she said. "There should be no double standards."

A year later, a judge in Georgia allowed a student newspaper to examine the records from a judicial board hearing on a fraternity hazing case but denied the newspaper's request to attend future meetings of the board. Mark Goodman, director of the Student Press Law Center, said that the First Amendment right to freedom of the press should overrule FERPA and force colleges to open up the records of the secret judicial board hearings.

"Universities are going to see that they can no longer stand behind it (FERPA) to cover up criminal conduct of their students," he said.[176] But state officials saw it differently. "I'm still not convinced that the behavior offenses we deal with are something the public needs to know about," said Alfred L. Evans Jr., senior Assistant Attorney General for Georgia. "The carryings on of fraternities here have more to do with drinking beer and acting ill-mannered than any criminal activity. I don't think college students should be publicly exposed for acting their age."

Frank LoMonte, the new executive director of the Student Press Law Center, said that colleges' misuse of the FERPA law to cover up crimes discourages the press, parents, and government from obtaining the information they need to evaluate programs and officials.

In its final days, the Bush Administration pushed through "ill-considered, eleventh-hour revisions" to FERPA that took effect January 9, 2009.[177]

"Because of ignorance, bad legal advice, or simply a desire to avoid public scrutiny, far too many school officials ignore the limited scope of FERPA and invoke the law to conceal anything and everything they can," said LoMonte. "Over-compliance with FERPA is so rampant and so widely documented that you'd assume the U.S. Department of Education, which is in charge of interpreting the Act, would take every opportunity to clarify that the law should be applied narrowly. Sadly, DOE has taken the opposite approach. The department's new regulations are making FERPA even more confusing to administer—and when confused, schools inevitably err on the side of releasing nothing at all."

Under the rules passed by the Bush administration on its way out the door, even records with the student's name and identifying information blacked out can be withheld, he said. This results in campus police press releases that state things like "An unnamed person at an unnamed school on an unnamed date reported being robbed." When a school is locked down during a safety threat, he said, the new rules prohibit naming the school. They will now simply state that an "unnamed school" has been locked down for a terrorist threat. As LoMonte pointed out, this is a recipe for mass panic. The DOE has lost repeatedly when reporters who sought records were denied by schools citing the FERPA law.

"In other words, DOE—having lost repeatedly in court—is attempting by rulemaking to make FERPA say what it doesn't," said LoMonte. All fifty states have enacted laws requiring schools to make their documents open for public scrutiny. Because FERPA flies in the face of that overwhelming national consensus, it should be given the narrowest possible interpretation—exactly the opposite of the approach taken by DOE. "If the DOE does not voluntarily remedy the damage it has done, a harsh wake-up call will be coming from the courts."[178]

6

When the Party Ends and the Tab Comes Due

In previous chapters we've seen how millions of unprepared, disengaged, and anti-intellectual high school graduates have chosen to attend party schools to enjoy five or even six years at adolescent playgrounds that have been designed for their enjoyment. Party school administrators who need to keep their classrooms filled to pay for bloated administrative salaries and a never-ending construction program have dumbed down their classes and inflated grades to retain as many students as possible, even if they don't want to learn anything. The schools' multi-million-dollar advertising and public relations campaigns are designed to attract as many students as possible and they directly target the kinds of students who want to purchase a degree but are not interesting in doing the work to earn one. Meanwhile, tuition increases at two or three times the inflation rate every year and parents pay it because they are uninformed about how dangerous college campuses are and how little education is actually taking place. They continue to pay the ever-increasing bills because they mistakenly think a college diploma is the key to success for their children.

Eventually, like all parties, the five-year party comes to an end. After five or even six years enjoying themselves at the country club campus, students don their black gowns, have their names called, and receive their diplomas. Parents breathe a sigh of relief that the days of paying all those expensive bills have come to an end. It is, parents think, liberation day and they get set for the fascinating and lucrative careers that their children were promised all those years ago when they took the golden walk. Within the next few weeks and months, however, they begin to suspect that something has gone very seriously wrong.

The final inconvenient truth about party schools is that, for the vast majority of students, the lucrative careers that party schools promised fail to materialize. It's only in the months after graduation that parents begin to suspect that party school administrators sold them some very expensive snake oil. A serious case of buyer's remorse sets in. Instead of a mailbox full of job offers for their children, they get the bills from predatory lenders and credit card companies demanding payment. It's the final, cruel switch. Long after the five-year party ends, today's young adults are suffering from the hangover of worthless diplomas and a job market flooded with poorly educated party school graduates forced to work at jobs that don't require a diploma.

The Student Loan Trap

When America's 1.2 million college graduates take off their caps and gowns each year, they face an average of $23,000 in student loan debt and $3,000 in credit card debt. This is the final bar tab for the five-year party. It means Junior has to pay the equivalent of a small mortgage payment each month. It's the beginning of the painful "great awakening" from the college dream and it's when parents finally understand how party schools took them for a very expensive ride. While the 2010 changes to the federal student loan program will help this problem by increasing Pell grants to low-income students and reducing the payments for student loans, the bloated costs of higher education will remain a significant problem until they are dealt with by college administrations.

In chapter two, we looked at the kickbacks that party school administrators were accepting from predatory lenders in exchange for allowing them to set up call centers where lenders pretended to be college employees. In addition, some colleges allowed lenders to put their names on the college's "preferred lender" lists that implied they were endorsed by the college. Students who complained to administrators about financial problems were simply handed a predatory loan application, even though the government loan programs usually offer a much better deal. Students look out loans to pay their bar bills and spend spring break in Cancun. In the month after graduation, however, graduates and their parents finally discover how high those payments are going to be and the decades it will take to pay them off.

A popular T-shirt worn by recent college graduates proclaims in bold, black letters "Property of Sallie Mae." It's no joke. Student loans from predatory lenders like Sallie Mae are like carrying around a ball and chain. Although many hope to be freed from debt by the age of thirty or forty, it's not uncommon to hear college grads say they will be paying into their fifties. And there is no escape. Miss a payment and you fall into default, which adds penalties and fees that can cripple you for life. Students can never escape from these loans, even if they declare bankruptcy.

"When you can't find a job or pay your student loans, college can seem like the Big Rip-off," *Fortune* magazine reported in 2002. "Twenty-eight percent of those surveyed by Nellie Mae [another student loan company, absorbed by Sallie Mae] had combined undergraduate and graduate student debt of more than $30,000, and for 22 percent, their loan payments ate up more than one-fifth of their monthly income."[179]

Taking out huge student loans and counting on large postgraduate salaries to pay them off, which is exactly the sales pitch that party school administrators deliver to unsuspecting students and their parents, used to make sense but increasingly does not work any longer, said economist Edward Wolff of New York University. "Whereas their parents experienced rising wages over their lifetime," he said, that is no longer the case for today's graduates. "So college may have been a bad investment."[180]

Millennial authors like Tamara Draut, Michael Collinge, and Anya Kamenetz have written entire books about recent college graduates who struggle to pay off their student loans and face a future with crippling levels of debt. Anyone who still doubts that going to college can ruin your life should take the time to read one of their books.

"Shaney," a graduate of the University of Arkansas interviewed by Draut, had $25,000 in student loans, just a little above average, but was unable to find a job two years after graduation. "She's begun to question the value of going to college and finds herself wondering whether it wasn't all a waste of time," Draut wrote.[181]

Even though she is generally in favor of students going to four-year colleges despite the heavy cost, Draut said that after three years of paying loans, some young adults are less likely to agree that the benefits of college make the debt worthwhile.

"Borrowing for college is a lot like buying a new car," she wrote. "By the time that great 'new car smell' wears off, so does the joy of owning the car."[182]

Alan Michael Collinge, founder of the political action committee Student Loan Justice and author of *The Student Loan Scam*, has shown how predatory lenders teamed with Congress and party school administrators to set up one of the largest loan sharking operations in American history, worth $90 billion as of 2008.[183] Instead of encouraging graduates to pay off their loans as soon as possible, as credit counselors advise, predatory lenders encourage graduates to default so they can load on fees and penalties that can double or even triple the amount to be paid back. Ralph Nader, commenting on the problem in 2006, said, "the corporate lawyers who conceived this self-enriching system ought to get the nation's top prize for shameless perversity."[184]

Collinge's website has drawn student loan horror stories from all over the country. Britt Napoli, for example, originally borrowed $30,000 to attend graduate school. Nearing age fifty, he has so far paid the bank $33,000 but still owes $70,000 and is worried that the bank will garnish his Social Security benefits after he retires. Another student, "Elizabeth" of Illinois, whose loan payments amount to $1,100 a month, wrote to him, "I feel like this is a form of loan sharking, where financial aid offices and higher education institutes are pushing students into a life of debt, while the student is under the assumption that they are bettering their quality of life by obtaining a degree, which, in my particular case, I will never be able to use."

"I'm going to die with these student loans," said "Lori," a thirty-three-year-old woman who took on $40,000 in student loans and works as a social worker in Manhattan, earning just $16,000 a year. Her $250 payments cover just the interest, not any of the principal on her loans.[185]

With the diminished job market brought on with the economic recession that began in 2008, graduates are finding it even harder to make their loan payments and are increasingly calling on Mom and Dad to bail them out before they go into default. Robert Shireman, director of the nonprofit Project on Student Debt, said an increasing number of recent grads won't be able to find any jobs at all but will have to continue to make their loan payments. Because college loans cannot be forgiven, even if the graduate declares bankruptcy, a default can mean doubling or tripling of the graduate's debt, ruined credit, wage garnishment, and a lifetime of harassment by loan processors.

"Children are coming out into one of the worst job markets God ever made and lugging with them all this debt," said Robert Allen, a father of three children in their twenties from Downington, Pennsylvania, who has co-signed his children's loans and is therefore responsible for paying them off if his children cannot. "The minute they start taking water on their credit, you're coming up in the gunsights of creditors."[186]

Student loans are specifically excluded from bankruptcy protection, so even if graduates declare bankruptcy, their student loans are immortal and will follow them to the grave, no matter what happens to them. The constant harassing phone calls from collection agencies and the garnishment of their salaries and tax returns has led many debt-burdened graduates to consider suicide or moving out of the country. Collinge describes one student who moved to Southeast Asia to live his life productively without the huge cloud of debt hanging over his head.

Harvard professor Elizabeth Warren said Congress had given to the loan companies "powers that would make a mobster envious," including the ability to garnish, without court orders, salaries, Social Security, and even disability payments. They also included tax refund seizure, suspension of professional licenses, and termination of public employment. Many of these draconian measures, of course, make it impossible for students to make payments. What can you use to pay them back once you have lost your job?[187]

Many parents had not even considered the problem of paying back student loans when their children signed up for them. They simply assumed that what the party school administrators told them was true, that a child with a college degree would make enough money that it would not be a problem. Student aid counselors at colleges are notorious for minimizing the problem of paying back loans. About 70 percent of families didn't even consider their child's postgraduate earnings when they decided how much to borrow, according to a study of 1,400 students and parents released in August 2007 by student loan company Sallie Mae. Also, 40 percent said they paid no attention to the cost when deciding which college to attend.[188]

The Glut of Party School Graduates

The idea that there are thousands of corporate jobs waiting for brand-new college graduates as middle managers, researchers, and marketers is at least a decade out of date. American corporations have either phased out those kinds of jobs, sent them overseas, or transformed them into positions for temporary consultants. Any kind of job that can be performed over the internet, from radiological scan review to research to marketing, has been outsourced to third-world countries, where they cost companies only a fraction of what they used to pay here.

While a minority of the best college graduates are able to find jobs related to their intended careers, most of them, particularly the graduates of party schools and subprime colleges, have to settle for much less. What they can look forward to is what one author calls "crap jobs." They work in a cubicle at the minimum wage as a temporary employee with no benefits or are forced to accept jobs as pizza deliverers, mail carriers, clerks, and waiters. Jared Bernstein of the Economic Policy Institute estimated that in 2006 about 17 percent of jobs that did not require a college degree were held by college graduates and that there were seven million college graduates employed in jobs that did not require a degree.[189]

Most graduates of party schools have absolutely no idea how to find a job. During their college years, they never really chose a career and only chose a major when the college told them they could not put it off any longer. Then they chose their majors based on which department asked them to do the least amount of work. This lack of any kind of career direction fits right in with young adults' belief that luck will intervene and provide them with what they need when they need it. There was little understanding that the decisions they were making in college would have a direct impact on how successful they would become. They genuinely expect that recruiters from large corporations are waiting for them at the end of the graduation line to sign them up for $80,000 office jobs.

They have no idea how to write a resume or a cover letter. They have no idea how to dress or what to say at a job interview. They have little understanding about how the cool photo of them with their heads in the toilet bowl throwing up that they posted on Facebook will look to recruiters. They have no understanding that they will have to spend some time in the mailroom or some other lower level of the ladder and work their way up. They want to start at the top the day they are hired.

Party school graduates also have little understanding about how strongly their college's negative reputation will hold them back. After being burned numerous times by functionally illiterate party school graduates, employers are no longer impressed by a degree from We-Party-All-The-Time U. As part of its 2008 College Salary Report, the PayScale research organization looked at the difference in earnings between graduates of party schools and graduates of the best Ivy League schools. The researchers took the *Princeton Review*'s list of the ten top party schools and compared the numbers with schools like Harvard and Dartmouth in terms of average pay three years after graduation and twelve years after graduation. The difference between the salary of a graduate from a party school like Florida State and the salary of a graduate of an Ivy League school like Dartmouth was $51,000 after a dozen years, which would add up to $1.5 million over thirty years.[190]

Even before the economic meltdown in 2008, recent college graduates were having increasing problems finding any kind of employment. As early as the spring of 2006, the Bureau of Labor Statistics reported that there were simply not enough jobs for the new graduates. "Although college graduates have more job opportunities than groups with less educational attainment, their job opportunities have kept even less pace with population growth over the past sixty-one months than the job opportunities of the population in general," the Center for American Progress reported.[191]

By 2008, however, job prospects for college grads had declined even more, according to The Collegiate Employment Research

Institute at Michigan State University. "In two short years we have moved from a zenith of exuberant and aggressive college hiring, through a period of cautious optimism, to a place of quiet desperation." Of the companies included in the survey, 49 percent expected to decrease their hiring of new grads. "It's going to get worse," said Philip D. Gardner, director of the institute.[192]

By 2009, even college graduates who had secured jobs connected with their chosen careers were being laid off and unable to find new jobs. In New York City, for example, the number of graduates with bachelor's degrees who were collecting unemployment benefits had risen 135 percent in a single year. That rate was twice that of residents who had only a high school diploma.

"We have not seen this in prior recessions where there's been such an increase in well-educated people turning to unemployment insurance," said James Parrott, chief economist for the Fiscal Policy Institute. "It's an uncharacteristically well-educated group."[193]

Many of these party school graduates eventually enroll in community college programs that lead directly to well-paying careers as electricians, plumbers, nurses, medical records technicians, and computer technicians, but then they are paying for two educations: one that led nowhere and a second that trained them for a real job. In fact, the typical community college student no longer comes directly out of high school but is in the mid-twenties-to-late-forties age group seeking a fresh start in a new field. Community colleges have direct relationships with employers in the fields in which they provide training and certificates. Often, a community college graduate has a job waiting the day he or she receives a diploma.

Many professions that depend on a steady supply of eager young recruits to take entry-level jobs have already been hard hit by a generation that simply cannot afford to take a job with low pay. This includes social workers and especially teachers. Many millennials who planned to teach find they simply cannot afford to take a job that pays $28,000 a year when they are $20,000 in debt.

"We absolutely see a chilling effect (on public service professions)," said Robert Shireman, director of the Project on Student Debt. "Students are setting their sights on the future and saying 'I can't afford to be a teacher or a social worker.'" He found that 23 percent of public college graduates leave school with too much debt to repay their student loans manageably on a starting teacher's salary.[194]

Anthony Daniels was $58,000 in debt when he left Alabama A&M with a degree in education and was ready to start his lifelong dream of being a teacher, but when he did the numbers, he changed his plans and now wants to go to law school. "Unfortunately my situation is not unique," he said. "In fact, it is becoming the norm. We are losing too many qualified teachers because of student loans. It's not just a burden, it's a barrier."[195]

The problem can follow teachers for decades. Susan Knable, a forty-six-year-old special education teacher in Collins, Ohio, has $51,000 in student loan debt from acquiring her bachelor's and master's degrees a decade ago. A divorced mother of four, she lives in a rental apartment. If it had not been for the loan payments, which she said are like carrying a twenty-year mortgage, she would be able to afford a house. Each month, one of her paychecks covers her rent and her bills and the other paycheck goes to pay off her student loans. "I have a personal goal to get rid of that debt by age fifty, but I don't know if I'll make it. I might have to extend it to fifty-two." Her children have graduated from college and now they too have student loans.[196]

Another Ohio teacher, Terri Crothers, forty-four, owes $50,000 in student loans, despite having used $20,000 of her own money to pay her tuition bill. At the beginning of 2008, she was six months behind in her payments, and said she is kept up at night by the fear of going into default. "We're teachers and we're providing a public service," she said. "Since our pay certainly isn't keeping up, we could use help on this."[197]

The irony here is that many high school graduates were encouraged to enroll in colleges because party schools promised that they would earn higher salaries and live a more comfortable life. What they hadn't figured into the equation was the huge payments for student loans, which knock their net worth back below what they would have made if they had taken a job right out of high school.

The Bleak Lives of Party School Graduates

The crippling debt that party school graduates must deal with for decades after graduation has a devastating impact on their lives. The loans are always there, always getting in the way and keeping them back. It's part of every decision graduates make, from getting married, starting a family, and buying a house. Thanks to the unethical practices of the predatory loan companies and their close ties to party school administrators, student loans have in some cases become a lifelong burden that robs students and forces them into poverty.

A 2002 survey found that 14 percent of young adults had delayed getting married because of their student loan debt, 20 percent said they had delayed having children, and 40 percent said they delayed buying a house.[198]

In the four years it took to earn a business degree at Boston University, Tyson Hunter of Seattle ran up a debt of $152,000 in student loans. After graduation, he was hired by a market research company at a salary of $40,000 a year, well above what the average graduate makes right out of college. But his loan payments of $1,000 a month make up a third of his take-home pay. When he finally pays off his student loans, he will be fifty-three years old and will have paid $300,000 in principal and interest. To save money on rent, he has moved into his mother's condo.

"Buying a house? That's not even in the ten-year goals," he said. "The next two years are going to be crippling. Hopefully, after that, it won't be as crippling." Unless, of course, he should happen to miss a payment or send one in late. Then his loan will be in default and his $152,000 debt could double or even triple because of penalties and fees.[199]

Tamara Draut, director of the Economic Opportunity Program at Demos and the author of *Strapped: Why America's 20- and-30-Somethings Can't Get Ahead*, says our society has created a "debt-for-diploma" system that leaves graduates deeply in debt before they receive their first paycheck.

The one thing that all recent college graduates share, she said, is debt. "Young adults between the ages of eighteen and twenty-four have 22 percent higher credit card debt than those who were that age in 1989. Young adults between the ages of twenty-five and thirty-four are also deeper in debt. . . . In 2005, the average indebted adult under age thirty-four had slightly more than $8,000 in credit card debt." The most common reasons for the debt were car repairs, loss of a job, and home repairs and 34 percent reported using credit cards to pay for basic living expenses.[200]

"The rise in credit card debt, coupled with the surge in student loan debt, is the main reason why today's young adults are spending much more on debt payments than the previous generation," she said. On average, twenty-five to thirty-four-year-olds spend nearly twenty-five cents of every dollar they make on debt payments, despite the fact that most of them cannot even afford a mortgage.[201]

Krystal Grube, twenty-four, graduated in 2007 with $75,000 in student loans and landed a job in Boston, where she lives with her fiancé. Her $800-a-month loan payments exceed her share of her apartment rent and she will be paying them until the year 2040. As a result, she said, her options for fun are very limited and she is counting on getting a better job in the future to improve her lifestyle.[202]

Draut's own career has been influenced by the impact of her debts. At the age of thirty, she and her husband owed $57,000 in student loan debt and $19,000 in credit card debt. They found themselves sorting through their CD collection to find something to sell to raise enough money to buy food.[203]

In addition to dealing with crippling levels of debt, recent college grads have to deal with the reality that the dream jobs they sought might no longer exist. Grads stuck in "crap jobs" full of meaning-less drudgery and trapped in an office cubicle cling relentlessly to the fantasy that someday a man will call them on the phone and offer them their dream job after all. They often have a difficult time psychologically when they are forced to wake up and face reality. The dream job as a movie director, brain surgeon, wildlife biologist, oceanographer, or astronaut that party school administrators prom-ised would be waiting for them at the end of the five-year party is difficult to let go of, particularly for young adults who have always been told they are perfect and can "be anything they want to be." Often, it requires a push from Mom and Dad, who get tired of pay-ing off Junior's student loans and making contributions to the living expenses of their now thirty-year-old children.

Anya Kamenetz, author of *Generation Debt*, has become a spokeswoman for her generation. She said today's college graduates were told all their lives by parents and teachers to expect the world on a plate, but no one told them they were going to get stuck with the check.

She interviewed more than one hundred graduates for her book and was constantly surprised that so many young adults who had college degrees were working at jobs for which a high school diploma would have been adequate training. This would be bad enough, she said, but most of them were also paying crippling levels of student loan payments. These graduates have become, she said, "a generation whose unbelievably expensive educations didn't guar-antee them success, a sense of purpose or even a livable income."[204]

"Cindy," one of the students she interviewed, attended a four-year college in Georgia but dropped out when she got sick. Her $6,500 in student loans rose to $10,000 after she missed some pay-ments. She gets calls every week from bill collectors. "I regret with all my being having ever gone to college," she said.[205]

"Lagusta," another of Kamenetz's informers, operates a vegan catering company in upstate New York. She called college "a scam." She has $45,000 in college loans and said she would never have gone to college if she had had any idea how expensive it would turn out to be.[206]

"The college-for-all ideal doesn't serve young people and it doesn't serve the truth," said Kamenetz. "Post-high school training is a necessity. But it doesn't need to be an expensive hardship that takes the better part of a decade. . . . If more young people found their way to well-designed and highly focused vocational programs, we wouldn't be seeing the same delayed economic independence."[207]

Many of the millennials she interviewed have never held a job for more than two years, never had a full-time job, and never had a job that paid benefits. Kamenetz said the good jobs that colleges promised when they signed up have mostly disappeared or have been sent overseas. As full-time jobs have been eliminated, companies increasingly hire consultants or temporary workers for a special project or when business increases.

"Temporary and contingent employment is the second fastest-growing industry in the country," she said. "Manpower, the nation's largest temp agency, has more Americans on its books than Wal-Mart."[208]

Kamenetz's young informants are, as a whole, pretty miserable. Not only are they poor and in debt, but they feel that the promises that had been made to them about their futures have turned into major disappointments.

"A major source of career dissatisfaction for college grads is not the low salaries or the long hours, but the contrast between our bright, shiny expectations and reality," she said.[209] This is finally the day of reckoning for the products of the self-esteem movement, the day when "You can be anything you want to be" is finally discarded and replaced with "How the hell can I make enough money to support myself?"

Following your bliss, she said, can lead to economic disaster, unemployment, and a lifetime of debt. Instead of the high life, she said, many of her generation are leading what she called "the G lifestyle"—trying to live on $1,000 a month.

Instead of catching hold of the bottom rung of the corporate ladder and climbing their way up, as previous generations did, most recent grads take jobs for which they are usually overqualified and underpaid. They have no health insurance and no job security. Many of these jobs are temporary, separated by significant periods of unemployment.

"Today's job market is characterized by instability," wrote Draut. "Job security today isn't defined as knowing that you'll be at the company a year from now. It's knowing that you will be there *a month from now.* Young workers no longer start work at a company with the intention of staying until retirement. In fact, it's a stroke of good fortune if they'll still be on the company phone list two years later."[210]

Today 29 percent of young adults or 18.2 million nineteen-to-thirty-four-year-olds don't have health insurance, the age group with the lowest percentage of insured.[211] "In addition to often working in a benefit-free zone, moving up the wage or career ladder in the new economy is more difficult than it was a generation ago," she said. "The well-paying middle-management jobs that characterized the workforce up to the late 1970s have been eviscerated." Instead of permanent jobs, she said, millennials must accept temporary jobs where they are hired for a particular project and then let go.

"Paychecks may be sporadic and unemployment is always one project away," said Draut. "Instead of becoming more financially secure with each passing year, many young adults in their late twenties and early thirties find themselves struggling even more as they start having children and taking on mortgages. What they're experiencing is paycheck paralysis."[212]

The old idea that college graduates could afford to move into their own apartments after graduation has also changed in the era of party schools and huge student loan payments. Nearly half of college graduates move back in with their parents. Sociologists refer to this trend as "boomeranging" as the students who left home to go to college return because they are unable to find a job that makes enough money to support them, pressures that were unknown to previous generations.

According to the census of 2000, nearly four million people between the ages of twenty-five and thirty-four lived with their parents. Recent surveys have indicated that 60 percent of college students plan to live at home after graduation and 21 percent said they planned to remain there for more than a year.[213]

Wages for entry-level jobs haven't kept pace with inflation, but the real reason for this phenomenon is the crippling levels of debt that students have acquired by graduation. "It's become the norm for recent grads to move back home," said Alexandra Robbins, author of *Conquering Your Quarterlife Crisis*.[214]

According to the Bureau of the Census, 46.7 percent of women and 53.7 percent of men aged eighteen to twenty-four still live at home. For ages twenty-five to thirty-four, 14.3 percent of men lived with their parents, compared to 10.9 percent in 1960. According to the *Student Monitor*, 73 percent of today's graduating seniors will leave college with $23,000 in student loans and $2,169 in credit card debt.[215]

"Even before this latest downturn, this generation was not earning the same wages that their parents earned, taking inflation into consideration," said Robbins.

Recent graduates also suffer from a form of "cost shock" when they have to pay for the luxuries they took for granted. Students brought up with every kind of electronic toy from iPods to cell phones and expensive brand-name clothing were also coddled in college with private bathrooms, housecleaning services, twenty-four-hour food courts and state-of-the-art fitness centers. After graduation, for the first time, they realize the high prices they have to pay to maintain those luxuries.[216]

And although a previous generation of parents may have made threats like "As long as you live under my roof, you'll follow my rules," today's parents are much more willing to accept their children back, even into their thirties.

Most grown-ups do not look forward to continuing to live with their parents. "One of the prime reasons these 'boomerang kids' come back home is that housing costs have risen faster than inflation and faster than entry-level wages," said Draut.[217] Although the best places to look for jobs are big cities like New York, Washington, and San Francisco, those are also the places where apartments come with the highest rent.

"The conveyor belt that transported adolescents into adulthood has broken down," said Frank Furstenberg, the head of a MacArthur Foundation project studying the phenomenon. In the 1960s, kids were warned not to trust anyone over thirty. Today, they can't live without them.[218]

A *Newsweek* report on the problem said parents of boomerang children are uncertain about how long they should allow them to stay. "They're not sure when a safety net becomes a suffocating blanket. Psychiatrists say it's tough to convince a parent that self-sufficiency is the one thing they can't give their children."[219]

Has the "College Premium" Disappeared?

A generation ago, no one had any doubt that spending four years in college was an economic benefit. The Bureau of the Census calculated the "college premium" as being worth a cool $1 million over the course of a graduate's lifetime. Today, however, with the college curriculum dumbed down to grade school levels and tuition costs shooting up at three times the inflation rate, many economists and sociologists have advanced the heresy that, for many students, going to college may be an economic disaster.

Twenty years ago, Larry L. Leslie and Paul T. Brinkman, authors of *The Economic Value of Higher Education*, found that the college premium was alive and well. They concluded that for most people, private investment in higher education is a good decision; in many, probably most, cases it is an outstanding decision.[220]

More recent calculations, however, have found that the so-called college premium has faded or even disappeared. Jason Kovac of WorldatWork, a Scottsdale, Arizona, professional association, said the earning differential between a high school graduate and a college graduate has been compressed since 1975. In some cases, he said, "experience could mean as much as a college education, or potentially more." James Brennan, senior associate at the Economic Research Institute, said it was undeniable that the value of a college degree had depreciated in recent years. A degree, he said, merely signifies that the student has passed academic tests "with little relevance to the working world" and that employers understood that trade school graduates were much more focused on the specific skills that employers were looking for. "Today's bachelor's degree is yesterday's high school diploma," he said. "In an average family anyone can get one."[221]

Kim Clark, an education columnist for *U.S. News & World Report*, identified the problem more clearly. Although a degree from a prestigious college or university is likely to open the doors to employment, she said, graduates of party schools and subprime colleges are not getting what they are paying for.

"A wide variety of studies show that, on average, college pays off in financial and nonfinancial ways. But some college graduates, especially those who attend low quality institutions or take worthless courses, will be below that average and might very well be wasting their time and money," she wrote.[222]

The million-dollar benefit of a college education, she said, has shrunk to about $300,000 once the inflated costs of tuition and student loan interest are factored in. This calculation drew a number of comments from readers who suggested that a successful person will be successful with or without a degree. Bill Gates and many other wealthy dropouts have shown that it's the person and not the degree that determines success. And because smarter people tend to go to college, she said, it may be that the higher salaries earned by college graduates are due to this artificial selection and not because of any value added by their educations. Other readers told her that they thought their degrees were a waste of time and money because they did not earn anything near the $50,000 salary that the average bachelor's degree holder earns.[223] The student's major is a big factor in later success, she said. Those who majored in math, science, and career-related courses found better jobs than those who majored in English or history.

The U.S. Department of Labor has calculated that college graduates earn an average of $51,000 per year compared to high school graduates who earn just $31,000, but when you figure in the exorbitant tuition bills and the interest on student loan debts, the gap between the two is closing fast. What good is it to earn a $50,000 salary if you have to pay $800 a month in student loan payments? Also, it's important to remember that by the time students spend six years at a four-year college, their high school graduate classmates have already been in the work force making money and gaining experience for six years.[224]

Students are unlikely to make up the cost of tuition and loans, despite the higher salaries they earn, said *SmartMoney* columnist Jack Hough in 2009. The employer who requires a college degree is putting faith in a system whose standards are slipping. He knows he is preaching heresy here, but circumstances have changed since the days when the idea that everyone needed to go to college was first put forward. The years spent paying off a college graduate's loans, he said, puts him farther behind, despite higher pay, than a similar student who chose to go to work after high school graduation. It takes the college graduate years to catch up to the pay earned by the high school graduate.

"College degrees bring higher income," said Hough, "but at today's cost they can't make up the savings they consume and the debt they add early in the life of a typical student." While the high school graduate was busy earning, the college graduate was getting stuck with a huge bill.[225]

According to the Bureau of Labor Statistics, the advantage in wages that workers with college degrees hold over workers with high school diplomas hasn't risen significantly since the late 1990s. In 2004, the bureau reported that for the first time the number of college graduates who were unemployed was higher than the number of high school graduates who were unemployed.[226] The American Association of Economics found that the return on a college investment leveled off around 2005 with college graduates earning 45 percent more than high school graduates, but this estimate does not count the cost of paying off crippling college loans that high school graduates escape. Since 2005, the college premium shows signs of declining.

In September 2009, Korva Coleman of National Public Radio dared to ask a question that would have been absurd a generation ago: "If a college education doesn't always get you a job, but it almost always gets you in debt, is it worth going to college?" Richard Vedder, a professor of economics at Ohio University, was among those who answered "probably not." We are simply sending too many students to college and our economy simply cannot find appropriate jobs for them. "I think some kids are going to college that probably shouldn't go to college," he said. "It's becoming more and more difficult for new college graduates to get jobs, independent of the recession. Twelve percent of the mail carriers in the country have college degrees, and I have nothing against mail carriers with college degrees, but I don't think it's an absolute necessity to have a degree to carry the mail." He suggested that instead of pursuing the four-year college route, students should consider community colleges, career colleges, and vocational schools. "And some people, particularly those who are sort of, say, marginal academically anyway, perhaps it's a waste of money to go to a four-year school and run up a huge debt." Boyce Watkins, a professor of finance at Syracuse, told Coleman, "This blanket notion that going to college will guarantee you a better economic future is not always true."[227]

College Graduates Who Refuse to Grow Up

Among the many tasks that colleges used to perform—in addition to teaching students how to think, solve problems, and gather knowledge—was helping adolescents mature into adults. It used to be that during their college years students gradually assumed more responsibility for their actions and learned what our society expected of them as the leaders of tomorrow. They gained a greater understanding of how a democracy works and developed a system of ethics and morals that would guide their decisions in the future. Sadly, this is yet another task that party schools and subprime colleges no longer perform.

Students who received high grades for substandard work, who were taught that it's okay to break the rules and the law, and that their own pleasure was more important than being responsible, do not suddenly mature when they receive their diplomas. Instead, recent party college graduates have created an entirely new demographic group that refuses to grow up and attempts to extend the irresponsible party school lifestyle after graduation.

Sociologists have given this cohort various names, such as *adultolescents* and *twixters*, but they share similar characteristics. They live with their parents well into their thirties. They retain teenage interests in binge drinking, electronic toys, stylish clothing, and all-night parties. They work at a variety of dead-end jobs and switch employers often.

Journalist Lev Grossman, who invented the term *twixters*, said they inhabit "a strange, transitional never-never land between adolescence and adulthood in which people stall for a few extra years, putting off the iron cage of adult responsibility that constantly threatens to crash down on them."[228]

Sociologists fear that the machinery that turns young people into responsible adults has broken down. Faced with a culture that seems to have no morality and a marketplace that seems to have no place for them, they simply drop out and continue the hedonistic lifestyle that they developed in college. Life is an endless party.

"Parents were baffled when their expensively educated, otherwise well-adjusted twenty-three-year-old children wound up sobbing in their old bedrooms, paralyzed by indecision," wrote Grossman. Terri Apter, a psychologist at the University of Cambridge in England, said, "Legally, they're adults, but they're on the threshold, the doorway to adulthood, and they're not going through it."[229]

Developmental psychologist Jeffrey Arnett blames parents and a culture that planned out every step of these children's lives, from playgroups, Little League, and ballet through high school and the pressure to get into the best college possible. The years after college graduation, he argues, are the first time these children were allowed to think about their own lives and choose what they want for themselves. What may look like incessant hedonism, he said, is really a time to sort out their lives before passing through the one-way door to adulthood. It's not that they don't take adulthood seriously, he notes, it's that they take it too seriously.[230]

Party schools do nothing to prepare students for life after college and often contribute to the problem by giving students a very poor idea of how the world works. Any attempt to steer them in the right direction might encourage them to drop out and that goes against the prime directive: retention. Grossman said colleges are "seriously out of step with the real world in getting students ready to become workers in the post-college world." As an example, he cites Matt Swann, who took six and a half years to graduate from the University of Georgia with a degree in something called "cognitive science." Unable to find a job using his degree, he worked as a waiter and an insurance claims adjuster. "Kids used to go to college to get educated," said Swann. "That's what I did, which I think now was a bit naïve. Being smart after college doesn't really mean anything. 'Oh, good, you're smart. Unfortunately your productivity's shit, so we're going to have to fire you.'"

To a generation facing unprecedented levels of debt, adulthood begins to look more and more like indentured servitude, where even those who make a decent salary have to give it all back to the banks, leaving little extra for the little luxuries that make life worth living. The degree that was supposed to be the key to success and give them an economic advantage has been diluted by the fact that nearly 70 percent of high school graduates now go on to college.

There are plenty of Americans like Kate Galantha, who spent seven years attending four colleges and graduating with a degree in "undeclared" before taking a dizzying collection of jobs as a nanny, a wedding photographer assistant, a flower shop clerk, and finally an assistant at a photo studio. Each job was in a different city.[231]

Others think the unwillingness to grow up springs from pop culture, which celebrates youth and disparages old age. Advertising and movies aimed at young people celebrate the wonderful aspects of being young, but life seems to disappear when you reach the age of thirty. Why should anyone want to get old and accept responsibility? From the perspective of a twenty-five-year-old, it can look a lot like death.

Psychologist Jean Twenge, author of the bestselling *Generation Me*, ties the failure of college graduates to grow up directly to the self-esteem movement that taught them early that they could excel at anything they wanted. "Sooner or later, however, everyone has to face reality and evaluate his or her abilities," she said. Increasingly, for recent college grads, this day of reckoning can be put off until they reach the age of thirty, which, she said, many graduates told her is the year that adulthood begins.

"Twenty-somethings often take a while to realize that the 'Be whatever you want to be, do whatever you want to do' mantra of their childhoods is not attainable," she said. They are unprepared for the realities of the workplace, which often leave them confused and hurt by the harsh realities of their jobs. It's like a cruel joke, she said, that today's grads were raised to expect comfort and riches, but the reality is that they "can barely afford a condo and a crappy heath care plan."[232]

Psychologist Mel Levine, author of *Ready or Not, Here Life Comes*, calls the powerlessness that many college graduates feel in preparing for their first job *work-life unreadiness*. "Some emerging adults take longer to start up a stable work life than do others. Some never stop starting; they can't move ahead toward a career because of repeated false starts or because they keep changing course. They start up and then they stall out."[233]

Colleges do such a poor job of matching majors to careers, he said, that many students are unable to connect what they know and what they love with a job that will pay them a decent living. They are unable to make the connection between their skills and what is valued in the marketplace.

"We are in the midst of an epidemic of work-life unreadiness because an alarming number of emerging adults are unable to find a good fit between their minds and their career directions. . . . Because they are not finding their way, they may feel as if they are going nowhere and have nowhere to go."

Students who partied through high school and college are seeking the same kind of life after graduation, he said. "They just don't want to pull away from their teens. They may go after more and more education, move back with their parents, postpone tough career choices, and yearn for the intense group companionship that buffered their adolescence. The effects on work-life readiness may be catastrophic."[234]

How Parents Can Cancel the Five-Year Party

Parents who have read this far have a right to feel outraged about what irresponsible party school administrators with their eyes on the bottom line have done to much of higher education in America. Although the parents of the nation's 18,248,128[235] college students may think there is nothing they can do about it, they actually have tremendous power to force colleges to make reforms. The tuition money they help pay is what makes the party school system work. If they threatened to withhold it, party school administrators would listen. Similarly, as a powerful block of taxpayers, parents can insist that legislators make the policy changes that would help shut down the five-year party and prevent colleges from charging an ever-higher price for less and less education.

One of the reasons the party school system has been able to get away with it for so long is the cloak of silence administrators have thrown over so much of what they do, which keeps parents who pay the bills from getting a good look of what they are getting for their money. Year after year, parents pay an ever-increasing price for something they desire but which, to a large extent, no longer exists at most third- and fourth-tier state colleges. Armed with the information in this book, however, parents and taxpayers can fight back and demand reforms. The parents who pick up the tab for the five-year party can, and should, threaten to cut off the funds and put college administrators on probation until they abandon the irresponsible policies of packing their classrooms with disengaged students and force them to make education their prime focus, as it once was.

What is needed is a reinvention of higher education from the top down to reaffirm its traditional mission to educate young people to be the leaders of tomorrow. There is, in fact, a budding back-to-basics movement within higher education; its goal is to create "no frills colleges" where overpaid Donald Trump wannabe administrators are given pink slips and the over-built and expensive country club campuses would be scrapped. Projections from the few places that are working on this idea are that tuition could be reduced by as much as 75 percent.

Colleges need to be told bluntly that they are in the education business, not the entertainment business, and that too much tuition money is being wasted on administrative salaries, gourmet food courts, luxury dorms, hot tubs, and climbing walls. Education standards need to be raised to a level that guarantees a rigorous educational program and the accreditation organizations need to get tough in enforcing standards. Frivolous courses that are long on fun but short on education should be cut and replaced with rigorous courses in the core subjects necessary to maintain our economy, our government, and even the future of our country. Before they are granted a degree, students need to pass a "value added" exam proving that they have actually secured the minimum amount of skills and knowledge required to be a leader of tomorrow.

Parents and taxpayers should vote with their checkbooks and no longer write blank checks to colleges without a thorough examination of what they are getting for their money. Taxpayers should demand transparency for all college policies and proof that colleges are providing as much education as they claim. This chapter details specific steps that you, as a parent and as a taxpayer, can take right now to protect your child and cancel the five-year party.

How to Protect Your Child

1. Consider the alternatives to a four-year college.

For one of my two children, the college decision was easy. She was reading books before she went to elementary school and was clearly an intellectual in training, always wanting to learn about things and asking questions about how things worked and why. She went to the University of Rochester, a college she selected after months of making visits and reading reviews, and graduated with honors. Following in the footsteps of her journalist father, she now works as a blogger for *U.S. News & World Report* and is a frequent guest on television talk shows. Finding a place in the world for her was easy and she did most of the work herself, following a clear vision of what she wanted to do in her life.

For my son, however, finding his appropriate place in the world was not so easy. Early on it was clear he was not an intellectual. He did poorly in school in most subjects, was often frustrated when he was pushed by his parents, and always came out on the poor end when he was compared with his high achiever sister. It was pretty clear early on that he was not college material. Instead of accepting that, I continued to push him, which added to his frustrations and his sense that I was disappointed with him.

Tests showed that he was smart and he received great scores in math. He also had some talents that were hard to measure on tests. He had an infallible sense of direction and could give you specific directions to places he had been to only once years before. He was personable and well liked with lots of friends but usually kept his feelings to himself and it was never easy to figure out what kind of mood he was in or what he was thinking.

He spent a year at a community college but hated it and soon dropped out, much to my horror. He took a job as an orderly in a senior citizens home and was happy there, but it seemed like a boring career to me. Then, suddenly, he found his true calling, a career that made use of his talents and allowed him to make a successful living in a very unconventional way. He became a professional poker player. Today, he makes much more money than I do and works only a few days a month. His math skills, his poker face, and his excellent memory are all skills that he uses in his job and no one minds that he doesn't have a diploma to hang on the wall.

Looking back on this experience, I wish I had been more understanding and encouraged him to find his own way. I wish I had not tried to force him onto the college career path that he knew instinctively was not right for him. Pushing only made him more frustrated and damaged his self-esteem. My efforts to help were clearly counterproductive.

I am mentioning this because I think many parents make the same mistakes. Helping your child find the appropriate career path is one of the most important and most difficult tasks that parents face. I have spoken with many parents who were obsessed with getting their children into a four-year college, even when it was clear that their children were not intellectual and had no interest in further education. Our culture has constructed a hierarchy where four-year college students are at the top of the heap and students who attend community colleges or who take over family businesses or set out on their own are thought to be farther down in the pecking order.

College recruiters encourage this myth because it serves their own self-interest. They advocate sending every high school graduate to a four-year college because they think that's what parents want. It's important that parents realize that sending their children to college is not always the best option. There are other paths to satisfying careers that can lead to a fulfilling life without the decades-long burden of making loan payments for an expensive education that graduates never use. What parents should be looking for is the most *appropriate* option for their children and they, not guidance counselors or college admissions officers, are the ones best qualified to make that decision. There is no one-size-fits-all path to success. It's a little more difficult than that and it's important that parents understand what the other options are.

2. Have a serious talk with your children about their futures.

Perhaps the most important thing parents can do to avoid being fleeced by party schools is to take the time to make a reasonable and comprehensive evaluation of your child towards the beginning of eleventh grade. Don't automatically assume that a four-year college education is the best choice, even if the guidance counselor recommends it and a college recruiter attempts to sell you an expensive degree. The truth is that guidance counselors recommend college for 90 percent of high school students.

Our culture has a damaging prejudice against kids who opt out of the four-year college path, thinking of them as failures at the age of eighteen. As a result, parents face tremendous pressure to get their kids into college, any college, and party schools use this pressure as part of their marketing strategy to sell them a shoddy product at an inflated price. "Can't get your kid into a top college? Well, we want him at ours! And we cost less too. Step right up and sign here!"

Parents should take these advertising pitches with a grain of salt now that they have read the information in this book and know what really goes on behind the party school walls. A four-year residential college is only one of the paths to happiness and success and for many children it is exactly the wrong one. As we have seen in the previous chapters, sending the wrong kinds of children to college is dangerous and can lead to decades of financial misery.

The indisputable reality is that children have different talents, skills, interests, and abilities. Almost every child is good at something and among the important jobs of parents and teachers is to help children identify what they are good at and match it with the proper training to find a way to make a living using these gifts. Some students are good with their hands. Some can take a computer apart and put it back together. Some like to work outside. Some have social skills that make them good with people and some would rather read a book than go out and play. After seventeen years of observation, parents are the best possible real experts in evaluating their children's talents and abilities. Don't let guidance counselors, college recruiters, or party school administrators steer you in the wrong direction.

Some students should go to a four-college. If they like to read books, are curious about the world, like going to school, enjoy learning and acquiring knowledge, and have a specific career in mind that requires a degree, don't let anything stand in your way. Send that kid to the best college you can afford and rest assured that whatever you pay is worth every penny. Good colleges want these kinds of students and will be generous when it comes to financial aid. Just be sure you aren't wasting your money on a subprime party school that may look like a bargain but is really just an adolescent theme park.

At least half of American teenagers don't fit into the ready-for-college category and that's when parents have to make some hard decisions. Parents with highly inflated estimates of their children's intellectual abilities keep party schools in business. Sending educationally disengaged eighteen-year-olds to a subprime party school is dangerous and often does them more harm than good. These kinds of students can face decades of underemployment and crippling debt. About 1,700 college students die every year from alcohol-related accidents.[236] Remember that at party schools slackers make up the majority of students and they exert tremendous peer pressure on their fellow students to misbehave. Sure, these students will get a very expensive certificate, but they probably have not gained the knowledge and thinking skills that are supposed to go with it. As a parent, do you want to purchase an education for your children or do you just want a diploma? It's no longer automatic that the two things are the same.

When party school recruiters promise fascinating careers with high salaries for their graduates, parents need to remember that only the top 10 percent actually get there. For the vast majority of party school graduates, a college degree means being stuck in a low-paying job and saddled for years with tens of thousands of dollars of tuition loans. After reading this book, including the information in the appendix, you should have all the information you need to make a good choice as long as you are honest and open to the many options available. Remember that just because you can get your child accepted at a subprime college, it doesn't mean that is the best choice.

In my role as a teacher in a subprime college, I could tell on the first day of my classes which students should really be there and which were simply coasting along for the five-year cruise on the party barge. It should be even easier for parents to make this observation once they know what to look for. It's important to take a look at motivation as well as intellectual level. What does your child want to do with her life and why? Spending tens of thousands of dollars on higher education for a child who is not interested in education is simply tossing money away. It's like sending a vegetarian to an expensive steak house. Sure, you can just have the salad, but you're clearly in the wrong place. Sending the wrong kind of child to college is much worse than choosing not to go in the first place.

If your child doesn't read books, shows little interest in school, and often says he doesn't want to go, if he complains about doing his homework, gets in trouble at school and into disputes with teachers, if he spends most of his time with video games, web surfing, and partying with his friends, you are going to have to make some difficult decisions. Forcing this kind of child to go to college is asking for trouble. If your child acts like this with his parents and teachers carefully watching over him, what's going to happen in college with no one paying attention until he commits a crime or ends up in the hospital getting his stomach pumped? This happens every day at subprime colleges. Parents of these kinds of children assume that their children will grow up when they get to the campus, as if some kind of magical potion affects them over the summer when they turn eighteen. Believe me, it's not going to happen. Many of these children simply run wild when no one is around to make sure they follow the rules. Often, the only role models are older slacker students, who will provide the illegal alcohol and drugs, assistance in finding the next party, and instructions on how to cheat, plagiarize, and lie their way through college.

"The truth is there are students who are simply allergic to school," said Linda Lee, author of *Success Without College*. "They have to be monitored in high school to do their homework, they skip school, arrive late, leave early." College professors told her that three-quarters of their freshmen had no business sitting in a college classroom because they were spoiled, immature, and lazy and had no interest in studying what was being taught. From my twelve years as I college teacher, I agree completely. Many of my students even admitted to me that the only reason they were in college was to participate in the party or because their parents made them go.[237]

If, during the crucial conversation with your child, she says she wants to go to college, you need to ask her why. If she says she wants to learn, that's fine. If she says she wants to have a good time, you need to talk about other options. Neil Bull, director of Interim Programs in Cambridge, Massachusetts, told Lee that too many parents think they owe their child a college education, even if the child doesn't want one.

"I had this kid from Exeter," one of the top college prep schools in the country, Bull told Lee. "This was a wimpy, feckless child who got 1100 on his boards." This student had told his father he only wanted to go to college to have a good time.

"The father would be masochistically insane to send that kid to college," said Bull. "Most college freshmen are just falling-down binge drinkers."

"Would any sane parent spend up to $30,000 a year on a kid who said, straight out, that he just wanted to have a good time?" asked Lee. The answer, as I can attest, is that this happens every day with disastrous and costly results. "College is a very expensive way for your child to find himself," said Lee.

3. Consider community colleges, trade schools, or creative alternatives.

So what are the alternatives to sending your child to a four-year residential college? There are many options, but all of them suffer from a public relations perspective because they don't get as much attention as the glorified bachelor's degree route. It takes courage for a parent to "just say no" to party school recruiters and forge their own way.

Among the best and least publicized options are two-year community colleges, technical colleges, and trade schools, which are currently overflowing with students eager to get into them. Many of them now operate on twenty-four-hour schedules to accommodate all the students who want to attend. Unlike so-called liberal arts colleges, where students are left to make important career choices by themselves, these colleges are focused like a laser beam on specific careers and outcomes. When students choose a program, the college focuses on preparing the student for a specific career in such fields as nursing, computer repair, medical records technology, tax preparation, etc. Although these students also take classes in things like history and English, the classes are designed for the less intellectual, more practical individuals who make up a majority of their students. Best of all, however, are the close connections between the faculty and local businesses that will hire their graduates. Students who complete these programs have a direct connection to the employment market and usually have no problem finding jobs as soon as they take off their caps and gowns.

Two-year colleges also offer an important option. After graduation from a community college, students can pursue a bachelor's degree and transfer their credits to many four-year college programs at a considerable savings. This is a perfect route for students who are too immature to be left on their own at age eighteen but grow up significantly in their early twenties and decide that a bachelor's degree might be right for them after all.

Because most of these programs take only two years instead of four, they represent a huge savings when compared to a four-year school that is really a six-year school. Also, because they are often located close to home, students don't have to pay room and board and remain under parental guidance, unlike the freshmen who run wild on party school campuses. These students also have a much lower debt level than their counterparts from four-year schools.

Many parents say they are reluctant to take the two-year route, citing studies that show that the average four-year college grad makes more money than a community college grad. This gap, however, has been closing rapidly as four-year colleges increase their tuitions at two or three times the inflation rate and many holders of bachelor's degrees fail to obtain the white-collar jobs that are in short supply. Although the average plumber, electrician, or computer technician earns less than the average holder of a bachelor's degree, many technicians make much more than the average. Plumbers can move up to owning their own companies and have the potential to make more than the average college grad.

What parents have to battle here is our culture's bias against tech schools. We have been taught since we were babies that a four-year college is the goal and anything less than that is failure. Technicians, however, often find it much easier to get a job than college grads because their experience is needed everywhere and is easily transferable.

Another option is to set your child up in a business, either by starting one with the help of the Small Business Administration or purchasing an existing business or a franchise for a national company. For a tiny fraction of what it takes to send a child to college, you can set him up in his own business. If you choose the franchise option, the national company will provide the training and the support and your child can be an instant boss. This could be the key to an interesting future in that company or another, and even if it doesn't work out after a year or two, your child will be much more mature and wise to the ways of the world if you choose to send him to college after that. You could also set the child up in a storefront business in something he enjoys, such as clothing, jewelry, sporting goods, or baseball cards. Learning by doing is one of the best ways that young people today learn, and being in charge of something helps build maturity.

4. Consider enrolling your child in a "gap year" program.

Most American eighteen-year-olds are simply too immature to live by themselves. Studies have shown that today's teens are simply slower to mature than previous generations. In many other countries in the world, it's common for high school graduates to take a year off from school before college. In some countries in Africa, for example, college students are expected to spend a year in national service between high school and college. They can spend time in the military, work on public works projects, or join the merchant marine. In my experience, students who were only a year or two older than their peers in the traditional eighteen-to-twenty-one age group were much better students and stood head and shoulders above the crowd in terms of how much interest they showed in class. Their willingness to participate was also much better and they were much less subject to peer pressure from the slackers.

In Europe and Australia, there is a tradition of taking a gap year between high school and college, during which students take a break from formal education and come back with new experiences and a more mature attitude towards college. Sometimes this involves world travel and immersion in a foreign language or culture. Sometimes students take an internship to work in the arts or in anti-poverty agencies. Students can choose among such programs as learning to build guitars in England to caring for injured sled dogs in Canada. The practice has been resisted in the United States, apparently because it costs so much more to go to college here that parents are afraid they will lose their places in line. However, the practice seems to be catching on. In 2007, Princeton announced plans to send 10 percent of its incoming freshmen abroad for a year of social service before college.

Sabrina Skau, who graduated from high school in Portland, Oregon, in 2007, said she felt burned out after graduation and although she was a bright student with high test scores, she felt the last thing she needed right away was to go back to school. When she had the opportunity to teach English as a foreign language in Argentina, she jumped at the chance.

Professional college consultants, who are hired by parents to place their children in the best schools, are increasingly suggesting gap years as a way to avoid the expensive consequences of sending immature students to party schools. Stephen Roy Goodman, a consultant in Washington, told the *New York Times* in 2008 that there needed to be a better way.

"The bottom line is that almost 50 percent of students who begin a four-year college don't finish within five years and only 54 percent will graduate, even in six years," he said. "If that's the current rate, it's important you end up at a school where one, you're happy, and two, you're engaged and you want to learn."

Chris Yager, founder and director of Where There Be Dragons, a Boulder, Colorado, company that sets up gap-year programs, said the number of students who participated nearly doubled between 2007 and 2008, from forty-six to ninety-one. Students come back from these programs with unique knowledge and genuine self-esteem, unlike the false self-esteem they learned in school. Students have also learned to exist away from their parents, which is one of the stresses that college freshmen often have to face.

Emily Hadden from Tenafly, New Jersey, was able to defer her admission to Duke University for a year and moved away from her parents to a studio apartment in Manhattan, where she studied ballet. The year off gave her time to read books she had put off reading, mulling over possible careers and college majors, and generally taking a deep breath to contemplate who she was and where she was heading. When she arrived at Duke the next year, she said, it felt like taking a step backwards.[238]

5. Be skeptical and ask questions during college tours.

When parents, after considering all the options, decide that a four-year college is the right path for their children, they then need to make sure they are not falling into the party school and subprime college trap. Unfortunately, there are no signs at the college gates informing you that you're about to enter a party school campus. You have to do some homework. Readers of this book will be wise to the lies and deceptions that party school recruiters engage in to lure you into signing on the bottom line. It's just as important to be an educated consumer during college tours as it is in a car dealership showroom. Ask questions and get the answers in writing. Read the fine print. Many of these schools are hoping to squeeze as much money as they can out of you, so don't be an easy mark. Here are some suggestions for questions to ask and things to investigate:

- **Ask how many of the college's own professors send their children to school there.** In my visits to colleges around the country, I never ran into a single professor's child at a subprime party school. All of these professors lived within driving distance and it would seem like a wonderful opportunity. However, the more these professors knew about the colleges that employed them, the more likely they were to send their children elsewhere. They knew what went on there and they didn't want their children sexually abused in a fraternity house, getting their stomachs pumped for alcohol poisoning, or ending up with a valueless diploma.

- **Ask students you pass on the campus if it's a party school.** Believe me, they know, and they are usually proud of it. I have asked students this question at every college I have visited over the past three years. At party schools, students give you appreciative reviews of the party scene and will tell you how "awesome" it is. You could hear about the parties every night of the week if you wanted to spend the time to listen. If you asked a few more questions, you would find out that students "hardly have to do any work at all" and that "the teachers are really easy here. It's like heaven for students here." On the other hand, at places like the University of Virginia, Rensselaer Polytechnic Institute, or the University of Rochester, students insisted that it was not a party school or offered some qualifications like "we study hard and we party hard." At party schools, studying is not part of the deal. If you get any kind of doubt or hesitation from students when you ask the party school question, you are probably on the right track.

- **Go to the library computer lab and look over the shoulders of students to see what they are doing.** If it looks like research, intellectual inquiry, or even vague curiosity, that's fine. But at subprime colleges, you are much more likely to find students playing video games, watching YouTube, downloading pornography, or looking at profiles on Facebook and MySpace.

     At Florida A&M University at 10:51 A.M. on September 15, 2008, for example, a study by the student newspaper, the *Famuan*, found that fourteen out of twenty-seven computers on the second floor of Coleman Library were being used for

Facebook or MySpace. Other students who wanted to use the computers for research found that none were available and complained to the library staff that the computers were being misused. At party schools, the noncomputer sections of libraries—the places where rows of books are shelved—are usually ghost towns, devoid of students.[239]

- **Ask the college for documentation about how many graduates have found work in fields related to their area of study.** A decade ago, it used to be routine for colleges to conduct an extensive survey of their alumni and post this information on their web pages. If you do a Google search, you can find these old surveys of graduates dating back to the mid-to-late 1990s. Many elite colleges still take these surveys but hardly any party schools do it anymore. Why? It must be terribly depressing for party school administrators to watch the number of unemployed and underemployed students climb relentlessly year after year. There are just too many film majors who couldn't get jobs as documentary directors and too many theater majors working as waiters and clerks.

  In my own experiment, performed by tracing former students through their Facebook pages, I found that fewer than 10 percent of the students who graduated with journalism degrees found work in anything even remotely connected with journalism or public relations. I found a lot more of my former students working as clerks or waitresses five and even ten years after graduation. Good colleges are proud of their graduates and should be happy to supply you with information about them if you ask. Just watch out that you don't get overwhelmed with the 10 percent of excellent students who succeed despite the party school training. If you are shown a lot of profiles about specific students, ask about the averages.

- **If the college offers you a student aid package, make sure you get the offer in writing and make sure it's for all four years.** Many parents make the mistake of negotiating a beneficial aid package for their children, only to find that the offer only applies to the freshman year. This is a common enough problem that it has to be the result of a recognized policy. You can avoid this by asking about the other three years and adding it to the negotiated package. Make sure you get someone in the financial aid office to sign it.

- **Ask to visit a classroom in operation.** Make sure this is a random choice and not a class that was set up by the college with a model teacher and honors students. You can tell a lot just by observing what is going on. What is the attitude of the students? Are they asking questions, contributing comments, and paying attention? Or are they text-messaging, chatting with each other, eating, or sleeping? Is the teacher connected with the students or is she just lecturing remotely without any interaction with the students? Does she ask questions? Does she ask for comments? Another thing to look out for is the teacher who is playing the role of stand-up comic or quiz show host. Is actual learning taking place or is this just an entertainment exercise? Are the students running around the room playing musical chairs while the professor asks questions? If learning looks like it is taking place, it probably is. If the students aren't paying attention, they are most likely not learning anything.

- **Ask the town police and people in the community what students are like.** Most party schools have areas around the campus that the local communities call "dead zones." They are easy to spot because of the extremely run-down buildings with broken windows, grassless front yards, and mangled trees. There are often sofas in the front yards, beer kegs on the porches, and various forms of trash scattered throughout the neighborhood. These are high-crime neighborhoods with frequent assaults and arrests for underage drinking. The noise at night, even on weeknights, can be thunderous. These areas can become so overwhelmed with students that the parties spill out into the streets, blocking traffic. Conditions there are so bad that the students have driven away all of the non-students who used to live there, leading to further deterioration.

At my college, there were a number of these neighborhoods that were collectively known as "the ghetto." The streets looked like something out of a third-world country or sections of New Orleans after Hurricane Katrina. The area was obviously off-limits to housing inspectors. Students told me that the buildings were infested with rats, had holes in the floors, and that the staircases were unsafe. The college, of course, did nothing at all to combat the conditions there. They, too, looked the other way.

If you drive around the streets surrounding the campus, you are likely to come across these areas and you should take a good look. Is this the kind of place you want your child to spend a lot of time? Take a moment to get out of your car and chat with some of the local residents. Are there any residents who are not students? If so, ask them about the parties and how bad they are.

- **Investigate the underground cyberspace party school network.** Some high school students search the internet specifically looking for the least demanding colleges that welcome slackers. Sites like collegeconfidential.com, studentsreview .com, and vault.com offer insider information and peer review ratings directly from the students who are currently in college. The main objective is to identify and reject the more academically rigorous schools in favor of the subprime party schools where little work is required. Current college enrollees explain the real state of affairs to high school students who are weighing their options and want to find out which colleges are really party schools.

The online ratings are radically different from those published in college guidebooks and are probably more honest.

Prestigious schools with the best teachers and best programs, the ones that win high rankings in the published guides, are identified on the student-run websites so they can be avoided. They just demand too much hard work. What students who use these sites are looking for are easy classes, high grades for little work, no attendance policies, lots of fraternity parties, and little interference from administrators.

My college was described by "Handlebarsfsr," a student on ridemonkey.com, as: "Like the #2 party school in the nation. That place is liquor central." An anonymous freshman from my college posted on studentreview.com that she was "having the best time anyone could have." The classes were undemanding, she reported, and she could hand in her assignments two or three weeks late without any penalty. "Every night there is something to do. Walk outside your building and you can hear the frat parties bumping. You need to learn to balance your drinking and work but not really all that much. The work load doesn't ruin your life. You get it done and then you can go out, simple as that. The party nights to go out are Thursday and Saturday, the big parties where everyone you know is out, but other than that everyone goes out and it's a blast. They don't demand a lot from you and want you to have fun and get out and meet people instead of lock you in your room and make you study for hours upon hours. The place is definitely a party school so get ready to party. There are the kids who sleep in class and don't do anything and those are the ones you see sleeping over at the frat parties because they couldn't exactly make it back to their dorm."[240]

- **Have your child sign a FERPA release form.** This will allow you to examine disciplinary records, health records, and education records that colleges normally keep secret. Although some colleges place these forms in the admission packets, other colleges deny that they even exist, so you may have to be persistent. This is the best way to make sure you are in the loop when something goes wrong, but don't expect colleges to contact you. You need to check in every once in a while and if the college tries to stonewall you, produce the release form and demand access. Parents of students who died in college from alcohol poisoning told me they wished someone had told them about this.

Policy Changes That Will Help Shut Down the Five-Year Party

As taxpayers, the millions of parents of college students have significant lobbying power to force legislators to make the kinds of changes necessary to force college administrators to get out of the entertainment business and return to their rightful role in education. The following are policy changes that parents should encourage their lawmakers to enact. Even nonparents will benefit from these changes to ensure that their tax money is being spent on education and not the five-year party.

1. Cap college tuition increases at the inflation rate.

There is no reason colleges can't operate under strict budgets the way most government departments and organizations do. The cost of higher education has increased 439 percent since 1982, faster than health care or gasoline. Only 21 percent of this money is spent on anything directly connected with education. The other 79 percent is spent on building elaborate palaces with little to do with education and on administration salaries. Many colleges actually inflate their tuition rates to enhance their prestige. It's past time to get this under control.

State and federal governments could accomplish this by requiring colleges to cap their tuition rates or lose their state and federal aid. This would force colleges to be more efficient and use their

funding more creatively. They could also use more of their endowment funds for operating expenses. The current system that allows
colleges to increase their sticker prices at two or three times the
inflation rate is devastating to families and forces them to accept
high levels of debt. Cutting the sticker price would make it much
easier for students to attend and reduce the need for student loans.

In 2009, Pennsylvania began looking into setting up a no-frills,
back-to-basics college campus with no sports teams, no gourmet
food courts, no condominium-like dorm rooms, and no student
center. It was expected that tuition could be reduced by as much as
75 percent. Colleges should be encouraged to follow this example.

Another idea that should be considered is a three-year bachelor's
degree program. Hartwick College in New York began offering this
as an alternative in the fall of 2008. Students take eighteen credits
in the fall, four in a special January term, and eighteen credits in the
spring, to complete the 120 credits for their degrees. This simple
change can result in a tuition savings of $40,000.[241]

2. Require students who need remediation to get it before college.

A recent study found that 43 percent of community college freshmen
and 29 percent of four-year college freshmen required remediation
in math and reading, which cost $2.3 to $2.9 billion per year.[242] The
fault lies with high schools, of course, which granted diplomas to
students who had not yet reached the required levels of proficiency.
The best solution would be to stop the practice of graduating high
school students who cannot meet basic standards. It should not be
the college's job to bring these students up to speed.

Using college classrooms and professors to teach high school
algebra, reading comprehension, and basic grammar is a very
expensive waste of time. Worse yet are colleges that ignore the
problem and dump students in need of remediation into the general
population without any preparation at all. Many of these students

just get further and further behind until they drop out or flunk out, with debts as high as $50,000 and nothing to show for it.

A better way would be for states to set up special remedial programs at high schools for college-bound students in the summer before they go to college. Because the second semester of twelfth grade is often wasted, it would be the perfect opportunity to try again to re-educate these students in the basics. The high schools, which are often underused in the summer, would be the perfect location for these classes. It would even be worthwhile for parents to pay a part of the cost. That would still be a lot cheaper than college tuition. There should be rigid requirements and specially trained remediation teachers to deal with students who missed the basics the first time around. Colleges should administer a test to make sure incoming freshmen are up to speed and refuse admission to students who cannot pass it.

This would ensure that students entering college have a solid foundation on which to base their further studies, without worrying about their reading and math levels. It would guarantee that all college freshmen begin with the same basic skills and start out in the same place. Without this, many students enter college behind their peers from day one and never catch up.

3. Repeal FERPA and replace it with legislation that encourages parents to participate in their children's college educations.

It takes a family to build a college graduate. In the 1950s and early 1960s, colleges took much more interest in the personal lives of their students. There were enforced quiet hours, curfews, and rules about guests of the opposite sex. Students who didn't conform to specified moral standards could be expelled. Men and women sitting on a sofa, for example, were required to have at least three feet on the ground at all times. More seriously, colleges restricted what students were allowed to say and do on campus, which in the 1960s was justifiably found to violate their First Amendment rights. The idea of colleges acting as substitutes for parents dates back to English common law and is referred to by its Latin name, *in loco parentis*.

No one wants to go back to the repressive days of the 1950s, but clearly colleges have shifted too far in the opposite direction, taking little interest in what students do as long as they don't interfere with other students or the college. This "anything goes" attitude towards student behavior, which colleges refer to as *student empowerment*, has been a major contributor to the development of party schools. As was described earlier in this book, high school students who had their behavior carefully monitored in high school are suddenly dropped off at the campus and find that no one is watching them. The result is like a wild animal suddenly released from a cage. They go wild and often end up injured, in jail, or failing to attend any classes at all.

The majority of these students are simply not mature enough or wise enough to make decisions for themselves. Faced with the choice of attending a party or studying for a test, they make the wrong decision. Faced with the choice between drinking themselves into unconsciousness or stopping after one or two drinks, they make the wrong choice. Often, these wrong choices are dangerous, not just to the students themselves but to others. Clearly, what is needed is more guidance, control, and discipline, yet colleges claim their hands are tied by federal regulations that protect students' rights. Students treat this as permission to break all the rules with impunity.

A major step towards fixing the problems would be to change the regulations to require colleges to keep their students under control or share in the consequences of their students' actions, just as parents do. When a student is arrested for drunk driving, for example, the college should be required to immediately put the student on probation, inform the parents, and require psychological counseling. If the college is aware of a problem student and does nothing about it, the college should be held legally responsible for negligence. Students who repeatedly break the rules should be expelled.

An important part of this change in direction would be the repeal of FERPA, which keeps parents out of the loop in the college disciplinary processes. Parents, many of whom are picking up the educational bills, have a right to know what their children are doing in school and should have a right to see grades, speak with teachers and administrators, and look at the records of all disciplinary and medical matters concerning their children. At the age of eighteen, students may be legal adults, but most of them are unable to make mature decisions about their own behaviors until they are well into their twenties. James Buckley, the author of the FERPA law, has himself called upon Congress to revise the law to prevent its widespread abuse by colleges that have misinterpreted it.

Parents have eighteen years of experience in dealing with their child and know what motivates him or her. Why shouldn't colleges be allowed to use that experience when planning students' educational programs? One of the major powers parents have is that of the purse string. If the child misbehaves, the parent can threaten to stop writing the tuition checks and require the student to leave the party and find a job. That is a powerful, simple tool that students would not be able to ignore.

Of course, Diplomas Inc. would fight this change because it would make their jobs much harder. The current laws allow them to do pretty much whatever they want because the entire process is conducted behind closed doors. This should also be changed. Just as the law requires municipalities to make their arrest and court proceedings open to the public and the press, colleges should be required to do the same. The outcomes of these proceedings would serve, as they do in the outside world, as a deterrent to other potential criminals. If there are three students per semester who are expelled for repeated alcohol abuse, that would serve as a great incentive for other students not to follow in their footsteps. Disciplinary processes conducted in secret have no deterrent value at all.

4. Get colleges out of the criminal justice business.

Allowing colleges to investigate, prosecute, and determine guilt or innocence for felonies like assault, rape, arson, and burglary is clearly a conflict of interest. Colleges' first priorities will always be protecting their reputations from the outside world. Obtaining justice for victims and punishing wrongdoers will always be secondary considerations as long as party school administrators are in charge. Why do we need a separate criminal justice system just for colleges? It's one thing to deal with issues like plagiarism and cheating on tests in this way, but it's quite another to deal with serious crimes like this. Communities in which colleges are located have police forces, district attorneys, judges, and juries whose main functions are to deal with crime. Why not use them? What sense does it make to treat the same crimes differently depending on which side of the college gates they are committed? And why should colleges be allowed to cover up crimes by keeping all information about them secret? Does this serve the needs of the victims or the college's interest in protecting its reputation?

College crime victims, especially rape victims, have been complaining for decades that it is difficult to obtain justice from a college judicial board where everything is done in secret, including the final verdict and the punishment. Community courts perform most of their activities in the open, where they can be covered by the press and included in community and national crime statistics. It's time to prevent colleges from covering up crimes in this way.

5. Require that colleges give parents honest information.

Readers of this book should no longer be surprised that Diplomas Inc. does its best to hide what goes at college campuses and to cover up damaging information. This should not be tolerated, especially at public colleges, which are subject to the freedom of information statutes. Even the campus crime reports, which are specifically required by federal law, are often a lot more fiction than fact. What would help parents make better decisions about colleges would be a uniform set of statistics that would immediately separate the party schools from the serious schools. There should be serious penalties for reporting erroneous information, such as placing the school on a special list for the dishonest for a year or two.

The information parents need would include honest statistics on how many students die each year, how many graduates are working in jobs in their chosen majors, the average salary level for each major, how many students were dismissed by judicial boards, how often the college awards grades of A and B, student scores on standardized tests, the results of the National Survey of Student Engagement, high and low and median SAT scores, number of graduates who are currently unemployed, average college loan debt and credit card debt at graduation, percentage of students who took out student loans, average administrative salary, number of administrative positions, and the amount of budget spent on instruction.

Now that would make identification of party schools pretty easy! They would stand out from prime colleges like a sore thumb.

6. Reform the process by which colleges and universities are accredited.

Colleges and universities are proud of their regional accreditation and often proclaim it right on their web pages. For outsiders, it seems to mean that experts have examined the college thoroughly and determined that it does what it says it does. But what does accreditation really mean? Not much, it turns out. The regional accreditation organizations that are supposed to evaluate the quality of education at our colleges and universities seem to have been soundly sleeping as the colleges dumbed down their programs, inflated grades, and turned themselves into entertainment centers. They are like Securities and Exchange Commission watchdogs, fiddling with forms while corporate raiders fleeced millions of Americans and Bernie Madoff set up his Ponzi schemes.

There are six regional accreditation groups in the United States, but they all work pretty much the same way. Colleges apply for membership and then become a part of the organization. The college and individual departments submit regular self-study reports about changes they have made and problems they are experiencing. The accrediting groups develop a book-length statement of standards that they use as a guide when suggesting changes in college policies, courses, and programs. The accrediting organization collects comments and can schedule site visits to take a look at individual programs or problems, and once every decade they do a comprehensive evaluation of each college.[243]

On the face of it, this should work, so why haven't they spotted the problems documented in this book? First of all, the accrediting organizations are made up almost entirely of academics, including many from the organizations they evaluate. It does little good to have party school administrators evaluate themselves. Why not let parents and state legislators, the ones who pay the bills at state universities, have a say in what goes on?

Second, their work is done in secret. None of the reports and self-study documents are required to be made public. The public is invited to file complaints against individual colleges, but these complaints aren't made public either. The accrediting group doesn't do it and the colleges are not prohibited from doing it but rarely do. If this begins to sound like Agriculture Department food inspectors tipping off the meat-packing plants before they show up, you understand what I am talking about. It's all just too cozy, hidden, and friendly and it provides little protection for consumers.

Most importantly, however, the accreditation reports that I have seen are guilty of not noticing the forest for all those trees. The investigators are trained to look for small problems such as a need for more faculty in a particular subject, a change in the requirements for a major, or whether individual courses fit into the mission of the college. Colleges spend a lot of time fighting with other colleges that want to offer competing programs and similar degrees. A lot of politics is involved. The evaluators put on blinders when it comes to the big picture. Although they interview students enrolled in the program, they don't contact graduates about what they have and have not learned. They don't talk to employers about whether the graduates were adequately trained to perform useful work. The minutes of the bimonthly meetings are filled with these kinds of petty disputes; the larger picture is not discussed.

No evaluation official ever asks if students are really learning anything at these colleges. In the documents I examined, the issue is not even discussed. The New England Association of Schools and Colleges, for example, has published its Standards for Accreditation that deal with several of the issues documented in this book.

For example, section 4.2 requires colleges to demonstrate "an effective system for academic oversight, assuring the quality of the academic program," but this was mostly an illusion. Whenever I complained about academic standards, I felt like I was crying in the wilderness. The academic standards were largely in the hands of the students. If they thought a class was too difficult for them, the administration ordered it to be dumbed down or cancelled. This is where the accreditation watchdogs should step in and defend academic standards against these pressures to dumb them down to accommodate disengaged students.

Section 4.7 requires that students completing a degree must "demonstrate collegiate-level skills in the English language." This is something of a joke. If this provision were enforced, there would be a 90 percent decline in graduates at most colleges. Many of the graduates I was familiar with did not even possess high school level English skills. This provision would be wonderful if it were enforced. Sadly, it is not and no one seems to care.

Section 4.19 requires that graduates "demonstrate an in-depth understanding of an area of knowledge or practice." What they are talking about here is the student's major, but few students meet this requirement either, unless we are talking about plagiarism or partying as an area of knowledge. Only the genuine students—the 10 percent who actually came to college to learn something—possessed anything like an "in-depth understanding" of issues in their majors. The rest were merely treading water.

Parents who have been burned by colleges should not hesitate to file a complaint with the accrediting organization, but it seems to me that these organizations, as they are currently run, are not likely to get involved in a detailed evaluation of subprime colleges and party schools unless there is a huge public outcry against them. It would require a complete about-face for these organizations to get involved. Meanwhile, the "accredited" tag will carry very little weight with anyone who knows what's really going on.

State education departments also have the power to take a close look at colleges and universities in their states, but they rarely seem to bother, leaving the accreditation up to the regional groups. Colleges, of course, never invite them to take a look. Taxpayers and legislators who want to solve the five-year party problem should ask the state to investigate what is being taught—and not taught—in their state's higher education programs.

7. Require college seniors to pass a "value added" test before receiving a diploma.

This is perhaps the most radical but most effective idea in this book, yet it would not require a lot of resources or time. A group of experts in each field would come up with a list of essential information and skills that they would expect all bachelor's degree holders to possess at graduation. This would go a long way towards assuring future employers that what they are looking at is a competent future employee and not someone who took the slacker track through college. Students, of course, would be expected to go beyond the basics, but this test would make sure they had a firm foundation in their area.

Just the idea that this test existed would go a long way towards improving the attitude of students at subprime colleges. When a student asks, "Why do I need to know this?" the professor would simply be able to say, "Because it will be on the test," and not have to go into a long discussion about what is on the syllabus and why. Flunk the test and you don't get a college diploma. That's simple and easy to understand.

Why is this not the case now? Because professors are very resistant. Some college majors have what are called capstone courses, where students are asked to demonstrate all of the skills and knowledge they have acquired during their college years, but few actually give an exam. The idea, passed on from the pre-subprime days, was that a college education was too diverse and individual to be measured in a test. But the test I am recommending would not show everything a student had learned but simply guarantee that a student had learned the basic minimum.

For example, English majors would have to demonstrate a mastery of the rules of the English language and be able to identify people like Chaucer, Longfellow, and Emerson. Chemistry majors would have to show an understanding of basic formulas and the periodic table of elements. History majors would need to know when the Civil War was fought, who won the Vietnam War, and who was the king of England during the American Revolution. This may sound ridiculously moronic, but believe me, the vast majority of today's college graduates would probably have a very hard time passing such a test.

A passing grade on this test would show that a student has actually acquired enough knowledge to claim the privilege of being awarded a bachelor's degree. It would send a message to employers that a diploma is more than just a piece of paper. Passing this test would do what a college diploma used to do—demonstrate that a certain level of skill and knowledge has been achieved. For colleges, it would protect the integrity of their diplomas and help put an end to the increasingly low regard that employers have for them.

For students, it would be an incentive to buckle down and really learn something during their time in college. For professors, it would be a basic outline of what to teach in their classes, yet not so restrictive that it prevents them from making their own choices about what to teach. It would be a framework for what society expects its future leaders to know.

These tests already exist but are not used very much, probably because party schools don't want the public to know how little students are learning. To ensure that students in different colleges take the same test, it should not be drawn up by the colleges but by an outside organization. Fortunately, an organization that does exactly this already exists: the College Board, which administrates the SAT tests across the country. The new graduation exams could use the same format and methodology and could be graded the same way. The tests could be broken down into as many subgroups as necessary. Instead of one comprehensive English exam, for example, there could be separate exams for English and American literature. The state and federal governments could require these tests as a condition for receiving funding. Students who failed the test would take some additional classes at the college (which would make colleges happy) and be able to take the test again the next semester.

The same test should also be given to incoming freshmen, which would allow the college to measure exactly the improvement or "value added" students achieved during their college years. If a particular student's grade on the test rose from 56 to 86, the college could show that its programs added 30 points to the student's body of knowledge. Colleges could use these numbers to compare cohorts of students over time, compare the impact of new programs, and compare colleges to other colleges. It would provide solid information in an area that currently lacks it.

In the spring of 2009, colleges in Indiana, Minnesota, and Utah began this process by starting pilot projects in setting standards for what students must learn in various subjects. Supported by the Lumina Foundation for Education, the idea is based on the decade-old "Bologna Process," by which colleges in the European Union attempted to standardize what knowledge a diploma represented across various countries. The idea is to set quality assurance standards so that a diploma granted at one college means the same thing as one granted at another college.

While university catalogs describe the requirements for a degree in terms of the courses students are required to take, said Clifford Adelman of the Institute for Higher Education Policy, a listing of the number of course titles and numbers means nothing to employers or parents. The revised process would list specific categories of information that each graduate is expected to have mastered. "If you're majoring in chemistry, here is what I expect you to learn in terms of laboratory skills, theoretical knowledge, applications, the intersection of chemistry with other sciences, and broader questions of environment and forensics," Adelman said.[244]

A Call to Action

What is at stake here is the future of our country and its place in the world. U.S. college graduates, once the best in the world, currently rank twelfth among the thirty-five major industrialized nations, behind China, Canada, and South Korea, and other countries are catching up.[245] Unless we take action, the best American jobs will soon be exported to other countries, leaving our illiterate party school graduates to flip burgers and deliver pizzas.

Fixing American higher education's problems won't be easy. What it will take is a reinvention of colleges and universities, putting education and academic standards at the top of the list, and placing retention farther down. It will take a coordinated effort among parents, legislators, taxpayers, professors, and administrators. The first step, of course, is to admit that there is a problem, something that most academics have avoided doing for more than a decade.

The purpose of this book has been to inform parents about the abuses of higher education that party schools engage in to maximize the number of customers and their incomes at the expense of real education. It is my belief that informed parents are the best weapons to force college administrators and state and local governments to make the reforms necessary to ensure that colleges educate our children to the best of their ability. Parents and legislators, the ones who pay for higher education, hold the purse strings and can and should demand these reforms or threaten to withhold the funds that keep the party going. In return for their tuition money and education funding, parents and legislators should demand that colleges upgrade their academic standards, switch funding from frills to education basics, and guarantee that college graduates are proficient in the basic skills required to be employable and good citizens. They should demand solid proof that they are getting what they are paying for when they send their children to college—not just a diploma but a real education. Colleges need to call a halt to their outrageous tuition inflation, become more accountable, and pay more attention to affordability. We should settle for nothing less.

Appendix

The Red Flag List:
How to Spot Party Schools
and Subprime Colleges

Party schools and subprime colleges spend millions marketing their products to unsuspecting parents, but those who know what to look for can save tens of thousands of dollars by just saying no to the hype. The tips listed below are intended to be a consumers' guide for parents who want to avoid the party school trap. Parents can use it as a checklist to weed out the party schools from the colleges that still value education. If your college fails one or two of these tests, look more carefully. If it fails more than that, you may want to cross the school off your list and look elsewhere.

What a party school or subprime college IS NOT: It's generally not a top-tier school, as defined by the *U.S. News & World Report Guide to Colleges* or the *Princeton Review*. It's not a trade school, a vocational school, or a community college.

What a party school or subprime college IS: It's a relatively inexpensive four-year residential college/university that rates among the third and fourth tiers, as defined by *U.S.*

News & World Report. Not *all* third- and fourth-tier schools are party schools and/or subprime colleges, but most party schools come from this lower ranking level and admit students with low grades and SAT scores. These schools are, by nature, more interested in tuition money and keeping students entertained than education.

1. Student comments in college guides and rankings mention partying more than academics.

The *Princeton Review, U.S. News & World Report*, and student-run sites like studentsreview.com consist of a lot of statistics to help you determine what areas they specialize in. That's helpful, but none of these guides will tell you right out which ones are party schools. Take a look at the student comments, which are carefully selected by the editors to give a true impression of what the college is like. If students praise their teachers, talk about their classes, and discuss the learning environment, you are on the right track. If the students talk about how much fun it is, how you don't have to do any work, and how everyone parties all the time, you can cross that school off your list.

2. The school admits students with combined SAT scores of less than 1000.

Take a close look in the guides or on the colleges' websites at things like average SAT scores and the high school class rankings of incoming students. If the college admits students with SATs less than 500 in verbal or math, you are definitely in subprime territory. Few party schools have combined scores higher than 1050. Take a look at how many students come from the lower half of their graduating classes. That's a good sign that the college is not very picky about who they admit and probably doesn't care too much if they learn anything in college either.

3. More than 10 percent of the school's students require remedial programs.

Admitting students from the lower half of their high school class means they will need lots of remedial help in grammar and basic math skills, and that's a warning sign. You might be able to find out how many students are enrolled in these programs. If it's more that 10 percent, the college is probably admitting unprepared students to increase its bottom line. However, watch out if the college offers no remedial programs at all. They are most likely dumping the unprepared freshmen in with the other students, which is even worse.

4. More than 10 percent of the school's students are involved in fraternities.

The connection between party schools and fraternities is a symbiotic relationship. Party schools need fraternities to organize the kinds of illegal activities that attract students, and fraternities need party school administrators who will not crack down on them too hard. In fact, I don't know of *any* party schools that don't have fraternities. Students looking for party schools know this and look for colleges with lots of Greek activity. Many first-class colleges have banned fraternities because of their consistent illegal activities, including life-threatening hazing incidents, rape, and drug dealing. If fraternities seem to be at the center of most of the social activities on campus, it's a prime warning sign.

5. The college's view books make no mention of learning or teaching.

View books are the carefully prepared advertising brochures sent out by colleges to attract students. They can tell you a lot about the kind of student the college is trying to attract. Good colleges attract good students by promoting their teachers, classes, academic programs, and other aspects of education. Party school and subprime college view books feature students playing sports, eating in the elaborate food court, walking down the sidewalk, or enjoying the college's hot tubs, climbing walls, and workout centers. They avoid any mention of classes, studying, or teaching because they know that turns off the students they want to attract.

6. The college newspaper focuses on drinking and parties.

Most college newspapers are online and are a great resource for understanding not only what goes on there but what the students are interested in. As a former newspaper advisor, I was always surprised that more parents didn't take a look at the paper before enrolling their children. The paper clearly reflects the concerns of the students who write it and the students who read it. If the paper features "bars of the week" and advertises drink specials, that's a very good indicator that it's a party school. If every issue features articles about students being arrested, that's another sign. If there are any articles at all about classes, professors, or public affairs, that's a sign that it might not be a party school or subprime college.

7. The college covers up its real crime statistics.

There is probably no college statistic that is so deliberately and consistently falsified as the official crime reports. College officials apparently think that parents will believe the astoundingly low numbers posted on their websites. I have seen colleges report with an entirely straight face that only three assaults took place over an entire year at a ten-thousand-student campus. Outrageously low numbers are, in fact, a pretty good indication that the college is fudging the numbers. Instead of being fooled by this, it's a better idea to check with the watchdog group Security on Campus, which reports that only a third of colleges report crimes accurately. This group also includes reports of schools that were fined by the federal government for lying about crimes on their campuses. If they lied about this, you should ask yourself, what else are they not telling you? What else do they have to hide?

8. Students are making anti-intellectual comments on ratemyprofessors.com.

This site has a page for every college in the country on which students can comment about their teachers. This is a great place to find out whether students care at all about academics or are just looking for a place to hang out for five years. Pick a few professors at random and take a look at what the students are saying. Are these intelligent, helpful comments directing students to the best teachers or are they abusive, libelous comments about the teacher's clothing, sexual preferences, and grooming habits? At party schools and sub-prime colleges, the ratings are about who is the hottest teacher and who is most lenient about attendance policies, grading, and susceptibility to being coerced into awarding a better grade. Professors who attempt to maintain academic standards are regularly trashed at party schools.

9. Dormitory rooms are trashed by students.

The dorm rooms that colleges show off on the golden walk are carefully prepared false fronts. If you can arrange an unannounced visit, you can get a great idea about what life is like there. Such tours might be permitted on Parents' Weekend, for example. Look for overcrowding—a sign that the college is maximizing its profits by over-admitting customers. What you are likely to find in freshman dorms at party schools includes broken furniture, graffiti-covered walls, and vomit-filled bathroom sinks.

10. Police officers, firefighters, and EMTs are busy dealing with out-of-control students.

To avoid the college's public relations spiel, get the real story from the people who deal with day-to-day campus problems. It's worthwhile to make an appointment with off-campus first responders. When I was doing the research for this book, I was constantly astounded by the stories they told me about abusive, drunken students who refused to be taken to the hospital despite being unable to walk. These officials are the ones who are called to the campus to deal with drug overdoses and assaults, and to take unconscious, drunken students to the hospital. In party school towns, 60 to 80 percent of radio calls come from the campus. I've found these people very willing to give you the real scoop, especially if you tell them you are considering enrolling your child. Their job is to help people. College officials' jobs are to get you to sign up.

11. Students at sporting events are obviously intoxicated and obnoxious.

While off-campus drinking parties are usually off-limits to parents, sporting events are showcases for unruly students at party schools. Football tailgate parties at party schools feature hundreds of students drinking out of funnels and passing out while police stand by and do nothing. Many students don't even bother to attend the game. They're only there for the party. Basketball games feature hundreds of students shouting drunken obscenities while falling out of their seats. This is another place where you can see students in action without the admissions office's scripted tour.

12. Students in the library are playing, not doing research.

Libraries at subprime schools would have long turned into ghost towns if they had not been reinvented as computer centers. A quick tour is all you need to find out what students use it for. Are there students in the building or is it mostly abandoned? Are they using the computers to look up information for papers or are they using Facebook, MySpace, porn sites, and celebrity sites?

13. Students tell you their school is a party school.

In compiling the information for this book, I was surprised to find how honest and accurate students were when I asked them if they were attending a party school. They knew and they were proud. "It's a party school and everyone is ready to party" was a typical comment. At nonparty schools, however, students just laughed or said things like "I don't have time to party." I asked this question hundreds of times and I always found that the student comments matched everything I had learned about the college. It's an easy final test to see if the results match the answers you received on the previous questions.

Acknowledgments

A book is never the work of one person and this one is no exception. *The Five-Year Party* is really a collaboration of hundreds of people who understood that the abuses that were taking place on party school campuses needed to be stopped and that making the public aware of them was the first step to reform.

I have spent nearly forty years working with editors, but I never had a more talented one than Leah Wilson at BenBella Books. In addition to offering hundreds of suggestions to make this book better, she didn't hesitate to warn me when I was sounding too much like a curmudgeon and less like an investigative reporter. She drew up outlines for me to follow when my writing got disorganized and helped me eliminate thousands of words of great prose that were not appropriate for this book. Thank you, Leah!

My agent, Sally van Haitsma, understood how important this book was from the first time she read my book proposal. She helped me revise my proposal and was there to ride out the storm after publishers thought this book was too hot to handle. She also found me a great match with BenBella Books.

Elaine Ambrose took on the difficult task of fact checking the manuscript to make sure the information was accurate and attributed to the correct source. Any remaining errors are, however, the responsibility of the author.

My many friends and colleagues at Keene State College were helpful both before and after I decided to write this book by offering their views on party schools and what could be done about restoring rigor to higher education. I won't name them here because they asked me not to, but they know who they are. They're not just faculty but staff and even minor administrators who found it hard to sleep at night knowing they were part of the abusive culture that took advantage of students.

My colleagues at College Media Advisors, the professional association for advisors of student newspapers, were also helpful during the late-night sessions at the national conventions for nearly a dozen years where we discussed many of the issues in this book, particularly the efforts of colleges to cover up crimes and misbehaviors of administrators. For years, we discussed writing a book about this, and many of their ideas are included here.

Then there are my star journalism students, who were always among the 10 percent of students at party schools who really wanted to learn and were disgusted with the antics of the slacker majority. They could have gone to a better college but they stuck it out and I'm glad they did. Together, using the state Right to Know law, we exposed abuses that included lead paint chips in the playground of the college daycare center, toxic mold in dormitories that was sending students to the hospital, students forced to stand outside in freezing weather to register for housing, and college pledge parties that included underage drinking and strippers. I love all you guys and you made me very proud to be your teacher, even though college administrators cursed us under their breaths. I wish you the best of luck in your journalism careers and whatever you plan to do in the future.

Most of the first draft of this book was written at the Hannah Grimes Center in Keene, New Hampshire, and I want to think the staff and administration who understood why I needed to be locked away in my office all those hours. Thank you, MaryAnn, Kristin, Josh, and Dan.

I also wish to thank the people who helped out by reading earlier stages of the manuscript and offering helpful advice for revisions. These include Jean Winter and Al Stoops.

There are also hundreds of academics and former academics around the nation who made comments on my blog, sent me e-mails, or discussed issues that are raised in this book. Adjunct professors who are paid a pittance but are aware of what is going on were particularly helpful in telling me incredible stories about administrators exploiting students. They are too numerous to mention here, but I would like particularly to thank Marty Nemko, Larry Syzdek, Miriam Tiscotti, Ingrid Tewksbury, and Bob Bowblis.

Endnotes

1. B.S. Sonner. "A is for 'Adjunct': Examining grade inflation in higher education" (Statistical data included), *Journal of Education for Business,* September 2000, Volume 76 (11): 5.
2. Jonathan Whitbourne. "The Dropout Dilemma: One in Four College Freshmen Drop Out. What's Going on Here? What Does It Take to Stay In?" *Careers and Colleges,* March 2002, <http://findarticles.com/p/articles/mi_m0BTR/is_4_22/ai_84599442/?tag=content;col1> (accessed February 16, 2010).
3. Maurna R. Desmond. "The Coming College Bubble?" *Forbes,* October 23, 2008, <http://www.forbes.com/2008/10/22/college-debt-loans-biz-beltway-cx_md_1023schools.html> (accessed February 16, 2010).
4. Jean M. Twenge. *Generation Me* (New York: Free Press, 2006), 117.
5. National Association of Student Financial Aid Administrators press release, February 5, 2009, available on the NASFAA website at http://www.nasfaa.org/publications (accessed February 16, 2010). See also Tamar Lewin, "Study Finds Public Discontent with Colleges." *New York Times,* February 17, 2010.
6. Lynn Olson. *The School-to-Work Revolution* (Reading, MA: Da Capo Press, 1998), 19. See also Mary Beth Marklein, "4-Year Colleges Graduate 53% of Students in 6 Years." *USA Today,* June 3, 2009.
7. Alan Michael Collinge. *The Student Loan Scam: The Most Oppressive Debt in U.S. History and How We Can Fight Back* (Boston: Beacon Press, 2009), 121–122.
8. Eric Hoover. "'Golden Walk' Gets a Makeover from an Auditor of Campus Visits." *Chronicle of Higher Education*, March 6, 2009, Volume 55 (26): A1. See also Jacques Steinberg, "Colleges Seek to Remake the Campus Tour." *New York Times*, August 18, 2009.
9. Matthew Quirk. "The Best Class Money Can Buy." *Atlantic Monthly,* November 2005, <http://www.theatlantic.com/doc/200511/financial-aid-leveraging> (accessed February 16, 2010).
10. David L. Kirp. *Shakespeare, Einstein, and the Bottom Line: The Marketing of Higher Education* (Cambridge, MA: Harvard University Press, 2003), 11–31.
11. Jeffrey R. Young. "Homework? What Homework?" *Chronicle of Higher Education*, December 6, 2002, Volume 49 (15): A35–37.
12. Kirp, 12–15.
13. Thomas Bartlett. "Your (Lame) Slogan Here." *Chronicle of Higher Education*, November 23, 2007, Volume 54 (13): A1.
14. Ibid.
15. Greg Winter. "Jacuzzi U.? A Battle of Perks to Lure Students." *New York Times*, October 5, 2003.

16. Marysol Castro and Jen Pirone. "Living the High Class College Life." *ABC News*, September 20, 2008, <http://abcnews.go.com/GMA/story?id=5846595&page=11>.

17. Thomas Bartlett. "Club Ed: This University Is at Your Service." *Chronicle of Higher Education*, July 4, 2008, Volume 54 (43): A1.

18. Ibid.

19. Desmond, "The Coming College Bubble?"

20. Jon Marcus. "Up, Up and Away." *The Boston Globe*, October 5, 2009, <http://www.boston.com/bostonglobe/magazine/articles/2008/10/05/up_up_and_away/> (accessed February 24, 2010).

21. Martin Salazar. "Faculty, Administration at War over University of New Mexico's Future." *ABQ Journal*, January 31, 2009, <http://www.abqjournal.com/cgi-bin/decision.pl?attempted =www.abqjournal.com/news/metro/3101313metro01-31-09.htm> (accessed February 24, 2010).

22. Eric Ferreri. "Bowles Orders UNC to Cut from the Top." *News Observer* (Raleigh, North Carolina), August 29, 2009.

23. Carol Frances. "Higher Education: Enrollment Trends and Staffing Needs." *Research Dialogues*, March 1998, Issue 55, <http://www.tiaa-crefinstitute.org/articles/55.html>.

24. Cary Nelson and Stephen Watt. *Academic Keywords, A Devil's Dictionary for Higher Education* (New York: Routledge, 1999), 40–41.

25. Arthur Levine. "How the Academic Profession Is Changing," *Daedalus*, Fall 1997, Volume 126 (4): 1–20.

26. Gabriela Montell. "As Economy Sours, Presidential Pay Draws Increased Scrutiny." *Chronicle of Higher Education*, November 21, 2008, Volume 55 (13): B3. <http://chronicle.com/article/As-Economy-Sours-Presidential/7891>.

27. Ibid.

28. Nelson and Watt, 91.

29. Elizabeth Redden. "Following the Money in New Mexico." *Inside Higher Ed*, April 2, 2009, <http://www.insidehighered.com/news/2009/04/02/unm> (accessed February 24, 2010).

30. Brad Schrade. "Tennessee College Bosses Cut Back on Travel." *Nashville Tennessean*, December 11, 2008.

31. Ibid.

32. Jilian Mincer. "State Budget Cuts Push Tuition Higher." *Wall Street Journal*, October 17, 2008.

33. Richard Vedder. *Going Broke by Degree: Why College Costs Too Much* (Washington, DC: AEI Press, 2004), xviii.

34. Ibid., 8.

35. Goldie Blumenstyk. "The $375-Billion Dollar Question: Why Does College Cost So Much?" *Chronicle of Higher Education*, October 3, 2008, Volume 55 (6): A1, <http://chronicle.com/article/The-375-Billion-Question-/26459/> (accessed February 16, 2010).

36. Associated Press. "New York AG Alleges Student Loan Corruption." March 16, 2007.

37. Ibid.

38. Collinge, 1–21.

39. Ibid., 13–18.

40. John O'Brien. "Cuomo Looking into Student Loan Marketing." *Legal Newswire*, October 12, 2007.

41. Collinge, 79.

42. Karen Arenson. "Columbia Fires Its Director of Student Aid." *New York Times*, May 22, 2007. See also Jonathan D, Glater, "University of Texas Fires Officer over Tie to Loan Company." *New York Times*, May 15, 2007.

43. Ibid.
44. Collinge, 89.
45. Ibid., 79.
46. Ibid., 83.
47. Ibid., 91.
48. Jessica Silver-Greenberg. "The Dirty Secret of Campus Credit Cards." *BusinessWeek*, September 6, 2007, <http://www.businessweek.com/bwdaily/dnflash/content/sep2007/db2007095_053822.htm> (accessed February 24, 2010).
49. Tamara Draut. *Strapped: Why America's 20- and 30-Somethings Can't Get Ahead* (New York: Doubleday, 2006), 110.
50. Marc Scheer. *No Sucker Left Behind: Avoiding the Great College Rip-off* (Monroe, Maine: Common Courage Press, 2005), 39. See also "Don't Leave College Without It." *Mother Jones*, March/April 2002; Robert D. Manning. *Credit Card Nation: The Consequences of America's Addiction to Credit* (New York: Basic Books, 2000).
51. Silver-Greenberg.
52. Ibid.
53. David Tirrell-Wysocki. "Study: Many College Students Over Their Heads in Debt." Associated Press, March 12, 2008.
54. Ibid.
55. Silver-Greenberg.
56. Eileen A. J. Connelly. "Mixed Blessing: Credit Card Reform May Shock Some." Associated Press, February 22, 2010.
57. Tamar Lewin. "Lawsuit Takes Aim at College's Billing Practices for Study Abroad." *New York Times,* March 9, 2008.
58. Ibid.
59. Jonathan D. Glater. "Inquiry of Study Abroad Programs Grows." *New York Times*, January 21, 2008.
60. *Declining by Degrees: Higher Education at Risk*. DVD, PBS Home Video, 2005.
61. Ibid.
62. Ibid.
63. Julie Johnson Kidd. "It Is Only a Port of Call: Reflections on the State of Higher Education," in *Declining by Degrees*, Richard H. Hersh and John Merrow, eds. (New York: Palgrave Macmillan, 2005), 195.
64. Dave Newbart. "'Dumbed Down' College Math Courses Ripped by U. of C. Prof." *Chicago Sun-Times*, January 17, 2003.
65. Lianne George. "Dumbed Down," *Maclean's*, November 7, 2008, <http://www2.macleans.ca/2008/11/07/dumbed-down/> (accessed February 24, 2010).
66. Mike Flatt. "We Pay Your Salary." *Spectrum* (SUNY Buffalo), Volume 55 (60): February 22, 2006.
67. *Declining by Degrees*, DVD.
68. Derek Bruff. *Teaching With Classroom Response Systems: Creating Active Learning Environments* (San Francisco, California: Jossey-Bass, 2009).
69. Sara Rimer. "At 71, Physics Professor Is a Web Star." *New York Times*, December 19, 2007.
70. Gene Hartley. "Pyro Professor Has a Blast." *KY3 News*, October 27, 2008.
71. Stuart Rojstaczer. "Where All Grades Are Above Average." *Washington Post*, January 28, 2003.
72. Ibid.
73. Alicia Shepard. "A's for Everyone! In an Era of Rampant Grade Inflation, Some College Students Find It Shocking to Discover That There Are 26 Letters in the Alphabet." *Washington Post Magazine*, June 5, 2005.

74. Max Roosevelt. "Student Expectations Seen as Causing Grade Disputes." *New York Times*, February 18, 2009.

75. Ibid.

76. George Kuh. "What We're Learning About Student Engagement from NSSE." *Change*, March/April 2003, 25.

77. While some schools post the results of the National Survey of Student Engagement on their websites, most colleges keep them secret and NSSE tends not to over-generalize about national trends. The figures I use here were calculated by James Côté and Anton Allahar's analysis of NSSE data from hundreds of colleges. See their *Ivory Tower Blues*, 9.

78. James Côté and Anton Allahar. *Ivory Tower Blues: A University System in Crisis* (Toronto, Canada: University of Toronto Press, 2007), 9.

79. Murray Sperber. "How Undergraduate Education Became College Lite," in *Declining by Degrees*, Richard H. Hersh and John Merrow, eds. (New York: Palgrave Macmillan, 2005).

80. Malcolm Gladwell. *Outliers: The Story of Success* (New York: Little, Brown and Co., 2008), 35–68.

81. Richard H. Hersh and John Merrow, eds. *Declining by Degrees* (New York: Palgrave Macmillan, 2005), 1.

82. Kuh, 23.

83. *Newsweek* Poll: 750 Adults Nationwide, Princeton Survey Research Associates, June 24–25, 1999.

84. Jeremy Rifkin. *The European Dream* (New York: Penguin/Tarcher, 2004), 27.

85. Barbara Ehrenreich. *Bright-Sided: How the Relentless Promotion of Positive Thinking Has Undermined America* (New York: Metropolitan Books, 2009), 59.

86. Lois Romano. "Literacy of College Graduates Is on the Decline." *Washington Post*, December 25, 2005. See also Doug Lederman, "Graduated but Not Literate." *Inside Higher Ed*, December 16, 2005, <http://www.insidehighered.com/news/2005/12/16/literacy> (accessed February 24, 2010).

87. Doug Lederman. "Graduated but Not Literate." *Inside Higher Ed*, December 16, 2005, <http://www.insidehighered.com/news/2005/12/16/literacy> (accessed February 24, 2010).

88. National Endowment for the Arts. "To Read or Not to Read: A Question of National Consequence." Research Report #47, issued November 20, 2007. Available online at <http://www.nea.gov/research/ToRead.pdf>.

89. Ibid.

90. Bob Thompson. "A Troubling Case of Readers' Block." *Washington Post*, November 19, 2007.

91. Associated Press. "Students near graduation often far from competent, study says." January 20, 2006.

92. Mark Bauerlein. *The Dumbest Generation: How the Digital Age Stupefies Young Americans and Jeopardizes Our Future* (New York: Penguin/Tarcher, 2008), 17–21.

93. Laurence Steinberg. *Beyond the Classroom: Why School Reform Has Failed and What Parents Need to Do* (New York: Benson Bradford, 1997), 44.

94. Côté and Allahar, 66.

95. Paul Trout. "Student Anti-Intellectualism and the Dumbing Down of the University." <http://mtprof/msun.edu/Spr1997/TROUT-ST.html> (accessed on December 10, 2007).

96. Ibid.

97. Sarah Palermo. "Police Prepare for College, Arrests Are Expected to Rise." *Keene Sentinel*, August 22, 2008.

98. Philip Bantz. "Police taking it to the streets." *Keene Sentinel*, September 2, 2008.

99. Stuart Rojstaczer. "Grade Inflation Gone Wild." *Christian Science Monitor*, March 24, 2009.

100. Clynton Namuo. "UNH Camp Included Lewd Skits, Nudity." *New Hampshire Union Leader*, December 15, 2008.

101. Kathleen Bogle. "Hooking Up: What Educators Need to Know." *Chronicle of Higher Education*, March 21, 2008, <http://chronicle.com/article/Hooking-Up-What-Educator/26465/> (accessed February 24, 2010).

102. Robert King. "Students Drinking to Pass Out." *Indianapolis Star*, November 8, 2008.

103. H. Wechsler. "Alcohol and the American College Campus." *Change*, July/August 1996,Volume 28 (4): 20–25, 60.

104. Karen Kellogg. "Binge Drinking on College Campuses." *ERIC Clearinghouse on Higher Education*, ED436110, 1999, <http://www.ericdigests.org/2000-3/binge.htm> (accessed February 19, 2010). See also John McCormick and Claudia Kalb, "Dying for a Drink." *Newsweek*, June 15, 1998.

105. Catrin Einhorn. "Minnesota Bill Would Ban Limitless Drinking Specials." *New York Times*, January 20, 2008.

106. Wikipedia entries on Beer Pong, Funneling, Beer Goggles, and Shotgunning (accessed January 2008).

107. Jeffrey Gettleman. "As Young Adults Drink to Win, Marketers Join In." *New York Times*, October 16, 2005.

108. Jeffrey Gettleman. "Brewer to End Sound-Alike Bar Game." *New York Times*, October 19, 2005.

109. Sarah Rodriguez. "Alcohol Marketing and Youth." *Berkeley Daily Planet*, April 1, 2009.

110. "Number of Penn State Student Visits to ER for Drinking Reach New High." *Gant Daily*, February 27, 2009.

111. Scott T. Walters and Melanie E. Bennett. "Addressing Drinking Among College Students." *Alcoholism Treatment Quarterly*, June 2000, Volume 18 (1): 61–67. Walters, a researcher at the University of Texas School of Public Health, regularly updates these statistics. See also Alcohol Policies Project, Center for Science in the Public Interest, Fact Sheet, March 2000.

112. Associated Press. "Colleges Crack Down on Binge Drinking." October 15, 2008, <http://www.cbsnews.com/stories/2008/10/15/national/main4523871.shtml?source=related_story> (accessed February 19. 2010).

113. Paul Steinberg. "The Hangover That Lasts." *New York Times,* December 29, 2008.

114. Center for Science in the Public Interest. "Binge Drinking on College Campuses." December 2008, <http://www.cspinet.org/booze/collfact1.htm> (accessed February 19, 2010).

115. Meredith Granwehr. "College Drinking: Out of Control." *Hartford Courant*, December 7, 2007.

116. "Hard-working freshman adrift in a sea of partying students." *Dear Abby*, October 8, 2008.

117. "Parents Fed Up with Party Schools." Nationwide Insurance news release, August 19, 2008, issued on marketwatch.com.

118. Jane E. Brody. "Curbing Binge Drinking Takes Group Effort." *New York Times*, September 9, 2008.

119. Marc Fisher. "On Campus, Legal Drinking Age Is Flunking the Reality Test." *Washington Post*, August 21, 2008.

120. Barrett Seaman. *Binge: What Your College Student Won't Tell You* (Hoboken, NJ: John Wiley and Sons, 2005), 151.

121. Susan Snyder. "Hate Crimes Up on Campuses, Group Says." *Philadelphia Inquirer*, November 15, 2008.

122. Ibid.

123. Stephen Wessler. "Summary of KSC Student and Faculty/Staff Focus Groups on Campus Climate." Fall 2005, 4–10.

124 Angela Montefinise and Perry Chiaramonte. "Dorm's Many Sex Cases." *New York Daily News*, July 13, 2008. See also Steve Lieberman, "Family Renews Charges." *The Journal News*, August 7, 2008.

125. Anne Matthews. "The Campus Crime Wave." *New York Times*, March 7, 1993.

126. Mary P. Koss, Christine A. Gidycz, and Nadine Wisniewski. "The Scope of Rape: Incidence and Prevalence of Sexual Aggression and Victimization in a National Sample of Higher Education Students." *Journal of Consulting and Clinical Psychology*, 1987, Volume 55, 162–170.

127. "Sexual Assault on Campus," a report by The Center for Public Integrity, December 2009, available online at <http://www.publicintegrity.org/investigations/campus_assault/>.

128. Alan D. DeSantis. *Inside Greek U.: Fraternities, Sororities, and the Pursuit of Pleasure, Power, and Prestige* (Lexington, Kentucky: University of Kentucky Press, 2007), 102.

129. Maki Becker. "Three Indicted in Binge Drinking Death." *Buffalo News*, April 1, 2009, <http://www.publicintegrity.org/investigations/campus_assault/>.

130. Howard Pankrantz. "Teen's Death Brings New Lesson." *Denver Post*, March 11, 2009; and Dirk Johnson, "Rift on Indiana Campus After Student Dies." *New York Times*, November 28, 2009.

131. Michele Tolela Myers. "A Drinking Death in a Fraternity House." *New York Times*, December 6, 2008.

132. Amy Augustine. "Seven Arrested in November NEC Hazings." *Concord Monitor*, March 6, 2009. See also Katie Zezima, "7 Students Pledging a Fraternity Are Burned." *New York Times*, November 22, 2008.

133. Jenna Russell. "Student's Death Sharpens Focus on Hazing." *Boston Globe*, October 26, 2003.

134. Peggy Reeves Sanday. *Fraternity Gang Rape: Sex, Brotherhood, and Privilege on Campus* (New York, NYU Press, 1992), 33.

135. Larry Brown. "Baseball Not Bombs." *The Equinox*, November 7, 2007.

136. "Game Day = Binge Day," *Indianapolis Star*, October 26, 2008.

137. Santiago Esparza and Christina Stolarz. "52 Arrested at E. Lansing Riot." *Detroit News*, April 7, 2008.

138. Ibid.

139. Paula Schleis. "Kent's College Fest Turns Rowdy." *Akron Beacon Journal*, April 25, 2009.

140. Curt Brown. "Was Force Necessary to Break Up Dinkytown Party?" *Minneapolis Star-Tribune*, April 26, 2009.

141. Joan Arehart-Treichel. "Mental Illness on Rise on College Campuses." *Psychiatric News*, March 15, 2002.

142. Sabrina Tavernise. "In College and in Despair, With Parents in the Dark." *New York Times*, October 26, 2003.

143. John Fauber. "Sticking Objects Under Skin Rising Among Troubled Teenagers." McClatchy News Service, May 6, 2008. See also John Fauber, "Method Detects Self-Injury: Teens Embedding Objects Under Skin." *Milwaukee Journal Sentinel*, December 4, 2008.

144. Associated Press. "Reporting of Underage Drinking Differs." March 23, 2009. See also Howard Pankratz, "Littleton Teen's Death Brings New Lesson in Alcohol's Risk."

Denver Post, March 10, 2009; Mara Rose Williams, "College Students' Right to Privacy Frequently at Odds with Parents' Need to Know." *Kansas City Star,* March 19, 2009.

145. Ibid.

146. Ibid.

147. Howard Pankratz. "Littleton Teen's Death Brings New Lesson in Alcohol's Risk." *Denver Post,* March 10, 2009.

148. Jill Riepenhoff and Todd Jones. "Secrecy 101: College Athletic Departments Use Vague Law to Keep Public Records from Being Seen." *Columbus Dispatch,* May 31, 2009.

149. Sontag, Deborah. "Who Was Responsible for Elizabeth Shin?" *New York Times Magazine,* April 28, 2002, <http://www.nytimes.com/2002/04/28/magazine/28MIT.html ?pagewanted=1>.

150. Tavernise.

151. Ibid.

152. Ibid.

153. Wikipedia entry on Seung-Hui Cho, <http://en.wikipedia.org/wiki/Seung-Hui_Cho> (accessed March 25, 2009).

154. Ian Urbina. "Report on Virginia Tech Shooting Finds Notification Delays." *New York Times,* December 4, 2009.

155. Sara Lipka. "Education Dept. Releases New Rules on Student-Privacy Law, Giving Colleges More Room for Judgment." *Chronicle of Higher Education,* December 9, 2008, <http://chronicle.com/article/New-Rules-on-Student-Privac/1398/>.

156. Ibid.

157. Ibid.

158. "Security On Campus, Inc., Hails Landmark Federal Ruling That Says Colleges and Universities Can't Silence Campus Rape Victims," Security on Campus, Inc., press release, August 4, 2004.

159. Ibid.

160. Nina Bernstein. "College Campuses Hold Court in Shadows of Mixed Loyalties." *New York Times,* May 5, 1996.

161. Ibid.

162. Ibid.

163. Ibid.

164. Howard Clery and Connie Clery. "What Jeanne Didn't Know." Available at Security on Campus website, <http://www.securityoncampus.org/index.php?option=com_content &view=article&id=52.&Itemid=71>.

165. Elizabeth Holland. "There's No Verdict Yet on Campus Crime." *New York Times,* January 7, 1996.

166. Ibid.

167. Ibid.

168. National Institute of Justice. "Sexual Assault on Campus." December 2005, <http://www .ojp.usdoj.gov/nij/pubs-sum/205521.htm>.

169. "Eastern Michigan University Agrees to Pay Largest Ever Clery Act Fine Of $350,000." Security on Campus press release, June 6, 2008.

170. "DiNapoli: SUNY Colleges Inconsistently Reporting Crime Statistics." Office of the New York State Comptroller press release, October 22, 2008.

171. Gene I. Maeroff. "The Media: Degrees of Coverage," in *Declining by Degrees,* Richard H. Hersh and John Merrow, eds. (New York: Palgrave Macmillan, 2005), 11.

172. Jay Mathews. "Caveat Lector: Unexamined Assumptions About Quality in Higher Education," in *Declining by Degrees,* Richard H. Hersh and John Merrow, eds. (New York: Palgrave Macmillan, 2005), 47.

173. Mark D. Soskin. E-mail sent to Jay Mathews, quoted in "Caveat Lector" in *Declining by Degrees*, Richard H. Hersh and John Merrow, eds. (New York: Palgrave Macmillan, 2005), 47.

174. Carol G. Schneider. "Liberal Education: Slip-Sliding Away?" in *Declining by Degrees*, Richard H. Hersh and John Merrow, eds. (New York: Palgrave Macmillan, 2005), 61.

175. "Judge Orders Release of Campus Crime Reports," *New York Times,* March 15, 1991.

176. "Judge Lets Paper See Hazing Files, But It Seeks More," *New York Times*, April 5, 1992.

177. Frank LoMonte. "Down the FERPA Rat Hole." *Lake County News*, March 19, 2009.

178. Ibid.

179. Noshua Watson. "Generation Wrecked." *Fortune*, October 14, 2002, <http://money.cnn.com/magazines/fortune/fortune_archive/2002/10/14/330029/index.htm>.

180. Ibid.

181. Draut, *Strapped*, 45.

182. Ibid., 96.

183. Collinge, chapter 1.

184. Ibid., 5.

185. Draut, *Strapped*, 96.

186. Sue Shellenbarger. "The Next Bailout: Your Adult Children?" *Wall Street Journal*, October 8, 2008.

187. Collinge, 17.

188. Shellenbarger.

189. Barbara Ehrenreich. *Bait and Switch: The (Futile) Pursuit of the American Dream* (New York: Holt Paperbacks, 2006), 242.

190. Louis Lavelle. "Party Schools: Lots of Fun but Little Pay." *Business Week*, October 1, 2008. <http://www.businessweek.com/managing/blogs/first_jobs/archives/2008/10/party_schools_1.html>.

191. Christian E. Weller. "Employment Opportunities for College Graduates Less Abundant." *Center for American Progress*, May 5, 2006.

192. Sara Lipka. "Economy Chills Hiring Prospects." *New York Times*, November 20, 2008.

193. Patrick McGeehan. "This Time, Slump Hits Well-Educated, Too." *New York Times*, April 4, 2009.

194. Cynthia Kopkowski. "My Debt, My Life." *NEA Today*, January 2008.

195. Ibid.

196. Ibid.

197. Ibid.

198. Draut, *Strapped*, 96.

199. Nick Perry. "Graduates Drowning in Debt from High Cost of College." *Seattle Times*, October 5, 2008.

200. Draut, *Strapped*.

201. Ibid.

202. Shellenbarger.

203. Draut, *Strapped*, 1.

204. Anya Kamenetz. *Generation Debt: Why Now Is a Terrible Time to be Young* (New York: Riverhead Books, 2006), 8.

205. Ibid., 38–39.

206. Ibid., 45–46.

207. Ibid., 86.

208. Ibid., 100.

209. Ibid., 118

210. Draut, *Strapped*, 61

211. Tamara Draut. "Address the Pain, Reap the Gain: Our Nation's Future Demands That Political Leaders Take Seriously the Economic Plight of America's Young." *American Prospect*, March 18, 2008.

212. Draut, *Strapped*, 74–78.

213. Peg Tyre. "Bringing up Adultolescents." *Newsweek*, March 5, 2002.

214. Megan K. Scott. "The Boomerang Effect." Associated Press, April 27, 2008.

215. Ibid.

216. Ibid.

217. Draut, *Strapped*, 13.

218. Tyre.

219. Ibid.

220. Larry L. Leslie and Paul T. Brinkman. *The Economic Value of Higher Education* (Phoenix, Arizona: Oryx Press, 1988), 181.

221. Mark McGraw. "Degrees of Value." *Human Resources Directory Online*, September 30, 2008.

222. Kim Clark. "Is a College Degree Really Worth the Cost?" *U.S. News & World Report*, November 17, 2008.

223. Ibid.

224. Perry.

225. Jack Hough. "The Case Against the College Degree." *Smart Money*, March 31, 2009.

226. Lev Grossman, "Grow Up? Not So Fast." *Time*, January 16, 2005. See also Adrienne Lu, "Degrees of Unemployment." *New York Times*, April 25, 2004.

227. Rebecca R. Ruiz. "Questioning the Return on Educational Investment." *New York Times*, September 3. 2009.

228. Grossman.

229. Ibid.

230. Jeffrey Arnett. *Emerging Adulthood: The Winding Road from the Late Teens through the Twenties* (Oxford: Oxford University Press, 2004).

231. Grossman.

232. Twenge, 102.

233. Mel Levine, MD. *Ready or Not, Here Life Comes* (New York: Simon & Schuster, 2005), chapter 1.

234. Ibid.

235. "College by the Numbers." *Boston Globe Sunday Magazine*, May 31, 2009.

236. National Institute on Alcohol Abuse and Alcoholism, "College Drinking, Changing the Culture," <http://www.collegedrinkingprevention.gov/StatsSummaries/snapshot.aspx> (accessed January 2010). See also R. Hingson et al., "Magnitude of Alcohol-Related Mortality and Morbidity Among U.S. College Students Ages 18–24: Changes from 1998 to 2001." *Annual Review of Public Health*, 2005, Volume 26, 259–79.

237. Linda Lee, *Success Without College* (New York: Doubleday, 2000), 9.

238. Alex Williams. "A Cure for the College-Bound Blues." *New York Times*, March 9, 2008.

239. Breanna Harvey. "Students Misuse Library: PCs Used for Fun, Not Work." *The Famuan* (Florida A&M University student newspaper), September 19, 2008.

240. Anonymous post by female freshman, studentreview.com, October 17, 2007.

241. Tamar Lewin. "An Option to Save $40,000: Squeeze College into 3 Years." *New York Times*, February 25, 2009.

242. Justin Pope. "Colleges spend billions to prep freshmen." Associated Press, September 15, 2008.

243. New England Association of Schools and Colleges (NEASC) Standards for Accreditation, Adopted 2005.

244. Tamar Lewin. "Colleges in 3 States to Set Basics for Degrees." *New York Times*, April 8, 2009.

245. "Education at a Glance 2009: OECD Indicators," a report by the Organization for Economic Co-operation and Development, available online at <http://www.oecd.org/edu/eag2009>.

Index

About the Author

Craig Brandon is a former prize-winning education reporter who spent a dozen years teaching journalism and advising the student newspaper at a four-year liberal arts college in New England. He is the author of five previous books and hundreds of articles for newspapers and magazines. His writing has won awards sponsored by the Charles Stewart Mott Foundation, the National School Boards Association, the New York State United Teachers, and the Associated Press. Craig won first prize in investigative reporting from the Education Writers Association. He lectures frequently on topics connected with his books and has appeared on the History Channel, National Public Radio, PBS, and *Unsolved Mysteries*.